FOREWORD BY LAURA SANDEFER

*The*
**MIRACLE**
**MORNING**
*for* TEACHERS

*Elevate Your Impact*
*for Yourself and Your Students*

HAL ELROD • HONORÉE CORDER

# THE MIRACLE MORNING FOR TEACHERS

Hal Elrod & Honorée Corder

Cover and Interior Design: Dino Marino, www.mybook.design

ISBN-13: 978-1-942589334

# DEDICATIONS

## HAL

This book is dedicated to all teachers. You have dedicated your life's work to positively influencing our future generations, and for that I deeply appreciate and honor you.

## HONORÉE

This book is dedicated to my family, first and foremost, and to all of the teachers out there, doing what you do for the love of doing it.

# CONTENTS

*A first look at the impact that a morning routine can have on the success of your students, inside and outside of the classroom. Learn how the Miracle Morning and the Life S.A.V.E.R.S. can be used to make them happier, healthier, and better adjusted.*

## Section I:
## The Miracle Morning + Life S.A.V.E.R.S

*The art and science of why mornings are the key to transforming both your life and your students' lives for the better.*

*How to actually wake up when the alarm goes off, going from being a snooze-aholic to an early bird in just five minutes.*

*What exactly will you do to maximize your mornings? Discover six time-tested practices guaranteed to elevate your consciousness.*

# Section II:
# The Not-So-obvious Legendary Teacher Principles

# Section III:
# The ABC's of Being a Legendary Teacher

# A SPECIAL INVITATION FROM HAL

Since 2012, readers and practitioners of *The Miracle Morning* have co-created an extraordinary community. Consisting of over 200,000 like-minded individuals from around the world, these people wake up each day and dedicate time to fulfilling the unlimited potential that is within all of us, while contributing to the collective Miracle Morning Mission—to *elevate the consciousness of humanity, one morning at a time.*

As the author of *The Miracle Morning*, I felt that it was my responsibility to create an online community where readers could come together to connect, discuss the book, share best practices, find an accountability partner, and support each other. I created The Miracle Morning Community as a Facebook group, since most of us are already on Facebook. This way you don't have to log into an additional website.

However, I had no idea that The Miracle Morning Community would grow to over 200,000 members and become one of the most positive, engaged, and supportive online communities in existence—but it has.

## Join The Miracle Morning Community on Facebook

I'm constantly astounded by the caliber and the character of our member community, which presently includes people from over 70 countries and is growing daily. I invite you to join us at **www.myTMMCommunity.com** (just make sure you're logged into Facebook).

More recently, the teachers who contributed to this book (you'll find many of their stories at the end of each chapter) are supporting each other in their own online community (for teachers only), where you can connect with other like-minded teachers who are reading and practicing *The Miracle Morning for Teachers* and implementing the Life S.A.V.E.R.S. with their students.

## Join *The Miracle Morning for Teachers* Community on Facebook:

To connect with other like-minded teachers, learn what's working, ask specific questions, share ideas and more, visit **www. TMMTeachersCommunity.com** (again, be sure that you're logged into your Facebook account to join the communities).

While you'll find many who are just beginning their Miracle Morning journey, you'll find even more who have been at it for years and who will happily share advice, support, and guidance to accelerate your success.

I'll be helping to moderate both communities and checking in regularly, so I look forward to seeing you there!

With love & gratitude,

–Hal

# FOREWORD

The first time I heard of Hal Elrod, I was driving 70 miles per hour up the I-35 on a hot, bright day. I was desperately in need of inspiration for a speech I was giving to teachers. How could I serve this courageous yet exhausted group of humans? What message would lift them up to feel encouraged for the sacred work they do?

I come from a long line of teachers and know intimately the exhaustion, stress, and feelings of scarcity that accompany the joy and ecstasy of being a teacher. There is never enough time, money, or energy to do what needs to be done.

My mind was whirling with memories. I was hearing my grandmother's voice saying, "Teaching is the highest calling." Then came my mother's voice as I pictured her slumped on the floor with tears streaming down her face: "I don't even have time to go to the bathroom during the day." And I remembered hearing her the very next morning as she gushed, "I wouldn't do anything other than be a teacher. It's more exciting to me than if I were a race car driver."

*This is the work of saints*, I said to myself as the trucks blew past. But it's so hard.

What do teachers need most? I can't solve issues of money or class size; neither, frankly, can I answer the complicated questions of how humans learn and what truly motivates young people to embrace the struggle of deep learning.

To get out of my mental wanderings, I popped on a podcast that a dear friend recommended.

It was an interview with Hal Elrod. His optimism, energy and belief in human potential hit me hard. *Wow, how can I bottle that and give it to every teacher on the planet?* Now that would change the world!

The next thing I heard shifted my life. It was the S.A.V.E.R.S. from his book *The Miracle Morning*. I had spent the past two years practicing getting up an hour before my children. My pastor had suggested this basic habit so I could grasp the sacred silence of morning before the noise of family and work erupted. I'd seen the power of incorporating morning mindfulness and rituals in my small school, Acton Academy. These simple steps added a joy and peace to our learning space, and the children embraced them with ease.

But what Hal presented was far more than just seizing some alone time and adding mindfulness into a school day. He had distilled a rich combination of six practices that were clear, user-friendly, and grounded in age-old truth and proven science.

I felt fueled for my message to teachers that day: *Let's begin with tapping into your own inner gifts and potential. By doing so, we regain our most powerful posture for working with children—that of curious, passionate learners ourselves.*

Since that fateful day on the I-35, I've practiced the Life S.A.V.E.R.S. every day. They make me feel strongly alive, which means I am a better person for the children in my midst, along with my family and friends.

While some people may focus on the word "morning" in this book's title, I focus on the word "miracle." This isn't magic. It isn't a recipe. It isn't a strategy. What you hold in your hands goes beyond those things. It does something supernatural: it brings life and healing where there was death and loss. It grows human potential, the least-accessed resource in the world. It turns the darkness of the morning into a miracle of lightness.

This book is a gift each teacher deserves. I'm excited for you to read it and treasure it as I have.

Laura Sandefer
Founder, Acton Academy
Author, *Courage to Grow*

# A NOTE FROM HAL

*In a completely rational society, the best of us would be teachers.*

−LEE IACOCCA

Welcome to *The Miracle Morning for Teachers*! What began as a book (*The Miracle Morning*) has become a global movement that is made up of millions of people from around the world who wake up every day and embark on a collective mission to *elevate the consciousness of humanity, one morning at a time.*

Though I may not know you personally, I think it's safe for us to say that there is at least one thing that you and I have in common (probably a lot more than just *one*, but at least one that we know for sure): *we want to improve our lives and ourselves.* This is not to suggest that there is necessarily anything *wrong* with us—or our lives—but as human beings, we were each born with the innate desire and drive to continuously grow and improve. I believe it's within all of us. Yet, most people wake up each day with their lives pretty much staying the same.

Whatever your life is like right now—whether you are currently experiencing extraordinary levels of success, happiness, and fulfillment; enduring the most difficult time of your life; or somewhere in between—I can say with absolute certainty that the Miracle Morning is the most practical, results-oriented, and effective method I have ever encountered for improving any—or quite literally **every**—area of your life, and doing so faster than you may believe is possible.

The Miracle Morning can be an absolute game-changer for teachers, allowing you to attain that elusive *next level* and take your personal and professional levels of success far beyond what you've achieved up until this point. While this can include advancing your career, writing a book, or even starting a business, it's often more about discovering new ways to experience deeper levels of fulfillment and success in aspects of your life that are important to you but that you may have neglected. This can mean making significant improvements with your *health*, *happiness*, *relationships*, *finances*, *spirituality*, or any other areas that are at the top of your list. In other words, this book isn't just about becoming a better teacher; it's about becoming a better *you*. By waking up each day and dedicating time to become the best version of yourself, your students will also reap the rewards.

Whether you want to make significant improvements in just a few key areas or you are ready for a major overhaul that will radically transform your entire life—so your current circumstances will soon become only a memory of what was—you've picked up the right book. You are about to begin a miraculous journey, using a simple step-by-step process that is guaranteed to transform any area of your life…all before 8:00 a.m.

I know, I know—these are some big promises to make. But *The Miracle Morning* has already enabled over a million people around the world to make profound changes in their lives, and it can absolutely be the one thing that enables you to create the most extraordinary life you can imagine. Honorée (whom you're about to meet) and I have done everything in our power to ensure that this book will truly be a life-changing investment of your time, energy, and attention. Thank you for allowing us to be a part of your life. Our miraculous journey together is about to begin.

With love & gratitude,

–Hal

# A NOTE FROM HONORÉE

*A good teacher can inspire hope, ignite the imagination,*
*and instill a love of learning.*
–BRAD HENRY

Good morning! I'm so glad you're here—and I'm betting it's an early morning when you're cracking this book open for the first time. I'm delighted to say you have no idea just how incredible your life is going to be when you embrace what you learn in these pages. And there is no way to predict the astonishing impact you will have on others by sharing what you learn in these pages with your friends, family, fellow educators, and, of course, your students.

But first, let me introduce myself just a bit. I've written dozens of books, and, in 2013, Hal and I met and partnered to co-create the first book in *The Miracle Morning* book series (*The Miracle Morning for Real Estate Agents*). I just celebrated my 2,150th day doing my Miracle Morning and the Life S.A.V.E.R.S., and it is those practices to which I attribute much of my success and overall happiness.

Up until now, I've been the business partner and series co-creator with Hal, working with our co-authors to write the books and quarterbacking the production of the books behind the scenes. This is the first one I've had the privilege to write—and what a privilege it has been! I share Hal's passion and commitment to elevate the consciousness of humanity, and *The Miracle Morning* is doing just that—one morning at a time.

When Hal suggested this book, I immediately loved the idea. I just knew this book could have the possibility of impacting current and future generations when it matters most—as young minds and hearts are developing, and while they are under the care of those who, in addition to parents, can make the most difference in their lives.

How I wish I'd been introduced to the Life S.A.V.E.R.S. at a much earlier age. There's just no real way to know how much better my life could have been. And while there's no benefit to spending too much time looking in my rearview mirror, there *is* benefit in making changes and upgrades when they are due! As substance abuse, addiction, and depression reach an all-time high in our world today (not just in our classrooms), doesn't it stand to reason that finding solutions is in order? And perhaps not the solutions that have become standard, but in their place, tried-and-true ways to *eliminate* pain and suffering and replace them with joy and success?

That's what *The Miracle Morning for Teachers* and the Life S.A.V.E.R.S. will provide for you—and anyone else who comes within the sound of your voice. Just imagine your own personal transformation; as you grow, you'll be better and better, in and out of the classroom. Your family and friends will enjoy the positive impact of your personal growth.

Your students—along with their siblings, parents, and other relatives—will benefit. Their other teachers will reap the benefits of having kind, centered, focused, and delightful students. Their friends will learn just by being in close proximity. Then, as they go out into the world as healthy, contributing members of society, your impact will continue to spread. Kinda cool, right? So cool! I hope you love reading and sharing this book as much as we've enjoyed writing it.

To your success!

–Honorée

# INTRODUCTION
# AND OVERVIEW

We're delighted you're here! What teachers do is nothing short of a miracle, and we've created *The Miracle Morning for Teachers* just for you—the teacher who wants more than just to punch a clock, teach a subject, and retire after thirty years.

You're here because you want—and are ready for—*more*. You want more from your teaching career. You want more *for* your students. You want more *from* your students. And you want more for yourself.

And that, our teacher friend, is why we wrote this book.

Turning the *Miracle Morning Mission* of *elevating the consciousness of humanity, one morning at a time* from a vision into a reality will require reaching the next generation, and then the next, and then the next. This won't occur while we wait (and hope) for them to *possibly* come in contact with *The Miracle Morning* or Hal in some happenstance way, but instead, by us engaging others with direct contact. Those on the front lines. Those who impact our children repeatedly and intimately.

Teachers.

Teachers became the answer when we pondered how to reach the next several generations in the most effective and impactful way.

Teachers are the perfect answer for several reasons. You interact with your students on a regular and often daily basis. You most likely became a teacher because you wanted to make a positive impact in the lives of our next generation. You are passionate about your subject and want your students to be passionate, too!

In order for that dream to become a reality, we realized a couple of things:

1. It is important to know and use something before it is taught.

2. The only way to discover what works is to try it, and keep working with it, until we've figured out what works.

So, we reached into the robust Miracle Morning Community on Facebook in the search for teachers who would be willing to conduct an experience and experiment with their students for an entire month. They had to be teachers who were already practitioners of the Miracle Morning and devotees to the Life S.A.V.E.R.S. themselves, so they were already ahead of the learning curve.

The response was positive and, frankly, overwhelming! We heard, *Yes, my students need this!* over and over again. The teachers who opted in were already using the S.A.V.E.R.S. in their own lives and were excited to adopt a process that they could share with their students.

Then, we wanted to know:

• Would the kids participate, embrace the Life S.A.V.E.R.S., and enjoy the process?

• Would incorporating the Miracle Morning practice into their classrooms make a significant difference?

The answers to these were also *yes*, as you'll see from the Legendary Teacher-Contributors who share their experience and results with you throughout this book (at the end of each chapter). We don't want to spoil it for you, but let's just say that the results were astounding and left no doubt in our minds that this book is needed now, more than ever!

To give you a sneak peek at what you can look forward to, here are a some of the teachers you'll meet throughout the book.

In Chapter 1, you'll meet Legendary Teacher-Contributor **Deborah Schaenzer**, who has been teaching grades five and six for over twenty-five years. She'll tell you that after her first month of practicing the S.A.V.E.R.S. with her twenty-eight students, the feedback was unanimous: "All twenty-eight [of my] students agreed that all teachers should be using the Miracle Morning."

- You'll also hear from **Angela McMillion**, a homeschool teacher for seven children. She explains why "the Miracle Morning is a powerful habit that enables students to feel a sense of control over their lives."

- In Chapter 2, you'll be introduced to longtime college math professor **Allison Dillard** and learn about the extraordinary improvement that the Miracle Morning has made for her students: "The results of our month of the Miracle Morning surprised me. The class's attendance and homework completion rates rose to over 90%, the highest they've ever been for my Pre-Algebra class." And share in her joy as she continues, "I absolutely love the Miracle Morning. It has helped me turn a boring math requirement that students take only because they have no choice into something that will positively affect the rest of their lives."

- In Chapter 4, you'll hear from a few of the students in **Deanna Perkins'** second-grade class. From Deanna's vantage point, when it comes to practicing the Life S.A.V.E.R.S. in her classroom, the most important thing is what her students think. So, what do they think of the S.A.V.E.R.S. in particular? One student, Ainsley, says, "My favorite part is meditation, because it lets my calmness spread around." Hollis says, "My favorite part is the vision board, because I get to draw what I want my future to be like." Samvi says, "I think it is awesome. It makes me ready for the day."

- In Chapter 7, you'll meet fourth-grade teacher **Jodi Fish** and discover the profound benefits of implementing the Miracle Morning in her classroom: "Incorporating the Life S.A.V.E.R.S. program into our morning meeting caused me to be more intentional about providing my students with a positive, calm start to our day of learning. It helped students let go of emotions and engage in learning activities. I noticed a more intense focus during instructional periods and more independence during work time." And she concluded, "Although I did tweak Life S.A.V.E.R.S. a bit to work for my students, there is only one thing that I would have done differently; I would have begun the S.A.V.E.R.S. on the first day of school!"

While these are only a handful of the more than a dozen Legendary Teacher-Contributors whom you'll meet throughout this book, we wanted to give you an idea of the profound benefits you can look forward to in your own life and in your classroom.

**How to Get the Most Out of This Book**

Whether you've read *The Miracle Morning* or not, everything you need to put your Miracle Morning into practice for yourself and your students is contained in this book and the accompanying free guide.

**First,** we invite you to take a minute now to join The Miracle Morning for Teachers Community (Facebook group) at www. TMMTeachersCommunity.com to get support and learn best practices from other like-minded teachers who are reading this book and implementing the Life S.A.V.E.R.S. with their students.

- **Second,** after reading this Introduction, we suggest that you skip ahead to "Chapter 10: The Miracle Morning 30-Day Life Transformation Challenge," read it, and begin your first 30-Day Challenge right away by simply implementing the "R" in S.A.V.E.R.S. (the "R" stands for reading). We're going to cover the Life S.A.V.E.R.S. in depth starting in Chapter 3, but for now, just know that you will already be doing the Miracle

Morning when you simply wake up and start your day by reading this book.

- **Third,** download the free *Miracle Morning for Teachers GUIDE* at www.MiracleMorning.com/TeachersGUIDE to get step-by-step instructions on how to lead your students through each Miracle Morning and show them how to conduct their first *Miracle Morning 30-Day Life Transformation Challenge* (after you've conducted your own 30-Day Challenge).

During your first thirty days, you'll complete this book (and possibly re-read it or start reading the next book on your list) and have a solid understanding of each of the Life S.A.V.E.R.S., as well as not only what makes a legendary teacher but how to become one yourself! Then, when you're ready to do your second 30-Day Challenge, you can include your students and follow the step-by-step Guide mentioned above.

**This book is divided into three sections:**

- Section I: The Miracle Morning & the Life S.A.V.E.R.S.

- Section II: The Not-So-Obvious Legendary Teacher Principles

- Section III: The ABCs of Becoming a Legendary Teacher

Included at the end of each chapter are stories from the Legendary Teachers who helped us share the Life S.A.V.E.R.S. with hundreds of students around the world. These stories will surely inspire and encourage you, along with telling you what worked (and what didn't), and these teachers can be the very first other folks you add to your teaching network.

This is truly a heart-centered project with the potential of all of us coming together to leave a legacy that will uplift, inspire, and truly change the world consciousness for the better. Starting with you, your classroom, and your students.

When you're ready, let's begin. *(Reminder: skip ahead to Chapter 10 and read it now...)*

# SECTION 1:

# THE MIRACLE MORNING
## +
# LIFE S.A.V.E.R.S

# — 1 —
# WHY MORNINGS MATTER TO TEACHERS
## (MORE THAN YOU THINK)

*You've got to wake up every morning with determination*
*if you're going to go to bed with satisfaction.*

—GEORGE LORIMER,
AMERICAN JOURNALIST AND AUTHOR

How you start each morning sets your mindset, as well as the context and direction, for the rest of your day. When you learn how to start every day with a peaceful, purposeful, disciplined, growth-infused and goal-oriented morning, you're virtually guaranteed to win the rest of your day.

Do you sometimes start your day feeling overwhelmed? I'd be willing to bet that many, if not *most*, teachers do. In fact, many don't even set an alarm clock. Their day starts when their eyes fly open in a panic as they remember everything they must do that day: planning lessons, helping students learn and understand new concepts, and even worrying about having to deal with behavioral issues and concerned parents.

What if you could have that hour of peace and quiet you've been dreaming about? That clean, uncluttered mental space where you could regain your sense of elegance and dignity, where you're in total control and can proceed in an orderly, self-nurturing fashion? But you think know you can't—or maybe you can *someday*, but not today. Maybe when you retire or move into a different role in the education system. Just not today.

It's no wonder that many teachers start their days with procrastination, letting the urgencies of the day set the agenda and sending a message to their subconscious that says they don't have enough energy, or even the will, to get out of bed. They think today will be another free-for-all where their personal goals go out the window in the usual scramble to meet others' needs.

Add to this the fact that most people create and reinforce self-imposed limiting beliefs by telling themselves that they are *not* early risers, so the pattern of procrastination shows itself before the day even starts.

What if you could change that?

What if, when the alarm clock starts beeping in the morning, you consider it to be life's first gift? It's the gift of time that you can give to yourself, dedicated to becoming the person you need to be to achieve all your goals and dreams—for yourself, your family, and even your students—while the rest of the world is still asleep.

You might be thinking, *All of this sounds great. But. I. Am. Not. A. Morning. Person.*

I understand. I really do! You're not saying anything I haven't told myself a thousand times before. And believe me, I tried—and failed—many times to take control of my mornings. But that was before I discovered the Miracle Morning.

Stay with me here. In addition to wanting to feel less stressed, more in control of your day, and less affected by what your students do and don't do, I bet you also want to stop struggling and worrying about having more month than money. You want to quit missing your goals and release the intense and not-so-great emotions that go along with those challenges. These things get in the way of being an effective teacher because they affect your self-esteem and prevent you from feeling great about yourself and your life.

I'm a firm believer in the advice given at the start of every airplane flight: put your oxygen mask on first, and then help your child. You won't be able to help anyone if you pass out due to lack of oxygen.

Many teachers don't see this simple truth. They think that success means putting their own needs last, and they have so much to do that they never get to those needs. Over time, they end up exhausted, depressed, overwhelmed, and even resentful.

Sound familiar?

Then know this:

*Mornings are the key to all of it.*

More important than even the *time* that you start your day is the *mindset* with which you start your day.

Although there's a possibility that you're reading this book after years of being a teacher, there's also a good chance that you're reading this book in the early stages of your life and work journey, which means that you may feel overwhelmed and seek answers. If that's the case, then practicing your Miracle Morning before anything else will ensure you get *your* time, uninterrupted. The good news is that it's worth it, and it is far more fun and rewarding than you might expect.

But, before I get into exactly *how* you can master your mornings, let me make the case for *why*. Because, believe me, once you've uncovered the profound truth about mornings, you'll never want to miss one again.

## Why Mornings Matter So Much

The more you explore the power of early rising and morning rituals, the more proof mounts that the early bird gets *a lot* more than the worm. Here are just a few of the key advantages you're about to learn how to experience for yourself:

## You'll be more proactive and productive.

Christoph Randler is a professor of biology at the University of Education in Heidelberg, Germany. In the July 2010 issue of *Harvard Business Review*, Randler found that "people whose performance peaks in the morning are better positioned for career success, because they're more proactive than people who are at their best in the evening." According to *New York Times* bestselling author and world-renowned productivity expert Robin Sharma, "If you study many of the most productive people in the world, they all had one thing in common—they were early risers." If there was ever an area of life in which being proactive and productive are crucial to your success, it's teaching!

You'll anticipate problems and head them off at the pass.

Randler went on to surmise that morning people hold all of the important cards. They are "better able to anticipate and minimize problems, are proactive, have greater professional success and ultimately make higher wages." He noted that morning people are able to anticipate problems and handle them with grace and ease. If you think about it, this could be the key to significantly decreasing the level of stress that inevitably accompanies being a teacher.

## You'll plan like a pro.

Planning is very important to legendary teaching. It's been said that *when we fail to plan, we are indirectly planning to fail.* Morning folks have the time to organize, anticipate, and prepare for their day—every day. Our sleepy counterparts default to being reactive, leaving a lot to chance. Aren't you more stressed when you sleep through your alarm, wake up at the last minute, and find yourself rushing to get out the door? Getting up before you *have to* lets you jump-start your day. While everyone else is running around trying (and failing) to get their day under control, you'll be more calm, cool, and collected.

## You'll have more energy.

One component of your new Miracle Mornings will be morning exercise, which often is something neglected by busy teachers (especially because the teaching day tends to start early). Yet, in as little as a few minutes, exercise sets a positive tone for the day—physically, mentally, emotionally, and even spiritually. Increased blood to the brain will help you think more clearly and focus on what's most important. Fresh oxygen will permeate every cell in your body and increase your energy, which is why teachers who exercise are in a better mood and in better shape, get better sleep, and feel happier throughout the day.

You'll gain early bird attitude advantages.

Recently, researchers at the University of Barcelona in Spain compared morning people—those early birds who like to get up at dawn—with evening people—night owls who prefer to stay up late and sleep in. Among the differences, they found that morning people tend to be more persistent and resistant to fatigue, frustration, and difficulties. That translates into lower levels of anxiety, rates of depression, and likelihood of substance abuse, but higher overall life satisfaction. Sounds good to me! A better attitude has helped me to create a more powerful mindset, which has made me a better human and has helped me be more effective, efficient, productive, and *kind*. All qualities that can and will help you be a better teacher, too!

The evidence is in, and the experts have had their say. *Mornings contain the secret to an extraordinarily successful life.*

## Mornings? Really?

I admit it. To go from *I'm not a morning person* to *I really want to become a morning person* to *I'm up early every morning, and it feels amazing!* is a process. But after some trial and error, you will discover how to outfox, preempt, and foil your inner snooze-a-holic so you can make early rising a lifelong habit.

Okay, sounds great in theory, but you might still be shaking your head and telling yourself, *I don't know if I can do it. I'm already cramming twenty-seven hours of stuff into twenty-four hours. How on earth could I get up an hour earlier than I already do?*

I ask the question, "How can you not?"

The key thing to understand is that the Miracle Morning isn't about denying yourself another hour of sleep so you can have an even longer, harder day. It's not even about waking up earlier. It's about waking up *better*.

Over a million people around the planet already live and swear by their own Miracle Mornings and have for years, some for over a decade. Many of them were night owls. In fact, when we surveyed members of The Miracle Morning Community, 72 percent indicated that they had "never been a morning person *before* they discovered *The Miracle Morning*." But now they're not only doing it, they're *thriving*. And it's not because they simply added an hour to their day. It's because they make that hour count. And so can you.

Still skeptical? Then let me tell you this: *the hardest part about getting up an hour earlier is the first five minutes*. That's the crucial time when, tucked into your warm bed, you make the decision to start your day or hit the snooze button *just one more time*. It's the moment of truth, and the decision you make right then will change your day, your success, and your life.

And that's why the first five minutes is the starting point for *The Miracle Morning for Teachers*. It's time for you to win every morning! When we win our mornings, we win the day.

In the next two chapters, I'll make waking up early easier and more exciting than it's ever been in your life (even if you've *never* considered yourself to be a morning person) and show you how to maximize those newfound morning minutes with the Life S.A.V.E.R.S.—the six most powerful, proven personal development practices known to man (or woman).

Chapters 4, 5, and 6 will reveal not-so-obvious legendary teacher principles related to accelerating your personal development, how you can structure your life to gain endless amounts of energy, and how to optimize your ability to stay focused on your goals and what matters most to you.

Finally, chapters 7, 8, and 9 cover the skills which, when mastered, will allow you to become the most incredible teacher you could ever hope to be. There's even a final bonus chapter from Hal that I think you are going to love!

We have a lot of ground to cover in this book, so let's jump right in.

## Meet Legendary Teacher-Contributor
# Deborah Schaenzer
### Grades 5-6, Tom McCall Upper Elementary School

Teaching is tough. Even as a teacher with twenty-five years of experience at the fifth- to sixth-grade level, I still find meeting the needs of my students to be challenging. Students with multiple ACEs [Adverse Childhood Experiences] (trauma) and learning disabilities are on the rise. Over a quarter of my students are English Language Learners, one of whom is a newcomer. Wanting success for my students, I am always looking for new ways to help them.

When I heard about *The Miracle Morning* and how it aligns with growth mindset and trauma-informed practices, I was convinced it would provide the help my students need.

My class's experience with the Life S.A.V.E.R.S. started at the beginning of the 2017 school year. Knowing I would be looping with this new group of fifth-grade students, I made the six-minute Miracle Morning S.A.V.E.R.S. part of our daily routine, knowing it would pay dividends in their sixth-grade year.

Unfortunately, when state testing started, our daily routine was interrupted, ending our S.A.V.E.R.S. as we headed into the last month of the school year. The difference in the classroom was obvious, even to the students. In their end-of-the-year reflections, students admitted to feeling more anxious and not "ready" for the day. Several wished the S.A.V.E.R.S. routine could have continued during the state testing time.

With the new school year, I re-established the six-minute S.A.V.E.R.S. practice with more than just an academic focus. This time, when creating their affirmations, we discussed who they wanted to be as a person, as well as a successful student.

The class easily fell back into the routine. Students created posters with definitions and details of what it takes to be successful. They looked at their own academic data and determined what they needed to improve. At the end of the month, students spent time reflecting on what worked for them.

Out of the twenty-eight students who completed the reflection, twenty-five found value in the S.A.V.E.R.S. and wanted to continue them for the remainder of the year. Multiple students shared that the Silent and Exercise times should be two minutes each, as those are their favorites. One student wrote, "I love the minute of silence. I can clear my mind." Another student wrote, "The exercise is awesome because I have a lot of energy and it helps me get rid of some of it."

All twenty-eight students agreed that all teachers should be using the Miracle Morning. One of my girls wrote that "getting back into this routine has helped me start my day off right."

Students want routines, and they want to know that they are more than just a test score. When the focus switched from just academics to who they wanted to be as a person, the changes were dramatic. Students began asking themselves, "Is this what a successful student would do?" Or, "Is this going to help me reach my goal?" Maintaining focus like this at such a young age would make for successful individuals in the future, and, after all, isn't that the goal?

## Meet Legendary Teacher-Contributor
# Angela McMillan
### Homeschool Teacher for Seven Children

I am a homeschooling mother to seven children, ranging in ages from three to fifteen. I am frequently looking for methods of engaging my children in new ways. *The Miracle Morning* really resonated with me because I've always felt that our best days of schooling happen when we get up and get going. It's easy to fall into a more relaxed routine at home when there isn't the pressure to start school at a certain time. The Miracle Morning routine helped me define, and meet, a personal standard for our home school.

One of the amazing things about the Miracle Morning routine for students is that children of all ages can take part. I was surprised when even my three-year-old was able to grasp what we were doing. She was willing and able to participate. She is a very lively, rambunctious child, yet her favorite activity seemed to be the Silence exercise. The Affirmations exercise was probably her second favorite.

My eleven-year-old son tends to become distracted in the mornings, and it wasn't uncommon for him to still be in his pajamas at lunchtime. The Miracle Morning completely changed that for him. The first time I noticed the change was the first Saturday after doing the Miracle Morning for a week. I had determined that I would just go through the exercises on our planned school days, which happened to be Monday to Friday. That Saturday, however, he got right up and completed all of the Life S.A.V.E.R.S. on his own. To top it off, he got dressed and ready for the day before I was even out of bed. I know he feels more accomplished when he sets his intentions for the day through his Life S.A.V.E.R.S. The Miracle Morning has brought a focus into his life that I had previously been unable to teach him.

The Miracle Morning has the potential to transform behavior in students. It is a powerful habit that enables students to feel a sense of control over their lives. I enjoyed witnessing the changes that became apparent in the lives of my students/children. They were more engaged in their schoolwork and even seemed to become more self-directed in some of their learning. I feel teaching them the ways of the Miracle Morning is one of the best tools I can give them to help them face their futures. It's a win-win when both the student and the teacher can learn and grow from the same daily exercises.

# — 2 —
# IT ONLY TAKES FIVE MINUTES TO BECOME A MORNING PERSON

*If you really think about it, hitting the snooze button in the morning doesn't even make sense. It's like saying, 'I hate getting up in the morning, so I do it over, and over, and over again.'*

—DEMETRI MARTIN, STAND-UP COMEDIAN

Have you ever considered that how we start our day could be the single most important factor in determining how we live our lives? When we wake up with excitement and create a purposeful, powerful, productive morning, we set ourselves up to win the day.

Yet most people start their day with resistance and procrastination, hitting the snooze button and waiting until the last possible moment to pry themselves out from beneath their cozy covers. While it may not be obvious, this seemingly innocent act may send a detrimental message to our subconscious. It programs our psyche with the unconscious belief that we don't have the self-discipline to get out of bed in the morning, let alone do what's necessary to achieve everything else we want for our lives.

Put another way, could it be that how we wake up in the morning impacts who we're becoming, and thus impacts every area of our lives?

When the alarm clock starts beeping in the morning, consider that as life's first *gift*, *challenge*, and *opportunity* to us—all three at the same time—each day. It's the gift of another day, the challenge of making the disciplined decision to get out of bed, and the opportunity to invest time into our personal development. It allows every single one of us to become the person we need to be in order to create the life we truly want. And we get to do all of this while the rest of the world continues to sleep.

However, if it weren't for this strategy that you're about to learn, Hal and I—and over a million other people—would still be snoozing through our alarm clocks every morning and clinging to our old limiting beliefs that we were *not morning people*.

The good news is that it is possible to love waking up—and do it easily each day—even if you've *never* been a morning person.

I know you might not believe it. Right now, you might think *that might be true for early birds, but trust me, I've tried. I'm just not a morning person.*

But it is true. I know because I've been there. I used to sleep until the last possible moment, when I absolutely had to wake up. And even then, it took me a while to get out of bed. I was a "snooze-aholic" as Hal calls them. I dreaded mornings. I hated waking up.

And now I love it.

How did I do it? When people ask me how I transformed myself into a morning person—and transformed my life in the process—I tell them I did it in five simple steps, one at a time. I know it may seem downright impossible. But take it from a former snooze-aholic: you can do this. And you can do it the same way I did.

That's the critical message about waking up—it's possible to change. Morning people aren't born; they're self-made. You can do it, and it doesn't require the willpower of an Olympic marathoner. I contend that early rising can become not only something you do, but a fundamental part of *who you are*, and you will truly love mornings. Waking up will become for you like it has for millions of others—effortless.

Not convinced? Suspend your disbelief a little and let me introduce you to the five-step process that changed my life. Five simple, snooze-proof keys that made waking up in the morning— yes, even *early* in the morning—easier than ever before. Without this strategy, I would still be sleeping (or snoozing) through the alarm(s) each morning. Worse, I would still be clinging to the false limiting belief that I am *not* a morning person.

And I would have missed a whole world of opportunity.

## The Challenge with Waking Up

Waking up earlier is a bit like running: you think you're not a runner—maybe you even *hate* running—until you lace up a pair of running shoes and reluctantly head out the front door at a pace that suggests you might be about to go for a run. With a commitment to overcome your seemingly insurmountable despise for running, you put one foot in front of the other. Do this for a few weeks and one day it hits you: *I've become a runner.*

Similarly, if you've resisted waking up in the morning and chose to hit the *procrastination*—I mean *snooze*—button, then of course you're not *yet* a morning person. But follow the simple step-by-step process that you're about to discover, and when you wake up in a few weeks (maybe even a few days), it will hit you: *OMG, I can't believe it...I've become a morning person!*

Right now, you might be feeling motivated, excited, and optimistic. But what happens tomorrow morning when that alarm goes off? How motivated will you be when you're yanked out of a deep sleep in a warm bed by a screaming alarm clock in a cold house?

We all know where motivation will be right then. It will likely have flown out the window and been replaced by rationalization. And rationalization is a crafty master; in seconds, we can convince ourselves that we need just a few extra minutes …

… and the next thing we know, we're scrambling around the house late for work, late for life. Again.

It's a tricky problem. Just when we need our motivation the most—those first few moments of the day—is precisely when we seem to have the least of it.

The solution, then, is to boost that morning motivation and mount a surprise attack on rationalization. That's what the five steps that follow will do for you. Each step in the process is designed to increase what Hal calls your Wake-Up Motivation Level (WUML).

First thing in the morning, you might have a low WUML, meaning you want nothing more than to go back to sleep when your alarm goes off. That's normal. But by using this simple five-step process (that takes about five minutes), you can generate a high WUML, where you're ready to jump up and embrace the day.

## The Five-Step Snooze-Proof Wake-Up Strategy

**Minute One:** Set Your Intentions *Before* Bed

The first key to waking up is to understand this: *your first thought in the morning is usually the same as your last thought was before you went to sleep.* I bet, for example, that you've had nights where you could hardly fall asleep because you were so excited about waking up the next morning. Whether it was when you were a kid on Christmas morning, or the day you were leaving for a big vacation, as soon as the alarm clock sounded, you opened your eyes ready to jump out of bed and embrace the day. Why? It's because the last thought you had about the coming morning—before you fell asleep—was positive.

On the other hand, if your last thought before bed was something like: *Oh gosh, I can't believe I have to get up in six hours—I'm going to be exhausted in the morning*, then your first thought when the alarm clock goes off is likely to be something like, *Oh gosh, it's already been six hours? Nooo…I just want to keep sleeping!* Consider that this is a self-fulfilling prophecy, and you created your own reality.

The first step, then, is to consciously decide—every night, before bed—to actively and mindfully create a positive expectation for the next morning. Visualize it, and affirm it to yourself.

For help on this and to get the precise words to say before bed to create your powerful morning intentions, download *The Miracle Morning Bedtime Affirmations* free at www.TMMBook.com.

**Minute Two:** Move Your Alarm Clock Across the Room

If you haven't already, be sure to move your alarm clock as far away from your bed as possible. If you use your phone as your alarm clock, put it on the other side of the room (or even on your bathroom counter). This will make it inevitable that you have to actually get out of bed and engage your body in movement to start each day. Motion creates energy, so getting out of bed and walking across the room naturally helps you to wake up.

Most people keep their alarm clock next to their bed, within reach. Think about it: if you keep your alarm clock within reach, then you're still in a partial sleep state after the alarm goes off, and your Wake-Up-Motivation-Level (aka your "WUML") is at its lowest point, which makes it much more difficult to summon up the discipline to get out of bed. In fact, you may turn off the alarm without even realizing it! On more than a few occasions, we've all convinced ourselves that our alarm clock was merely part of the dream we were having. (You're not alone on that one, trust me.)

By forcing yourself to get out of bed to turn off the alarm clock, you set yourself up for early rising success by instantly increasing your WUML.

However, on a scale of one to ten, your WUML may still be hovering around a five, and you'll likely be feeling more sleepy than not, so the temptation to turn around and crawl back into bed will still be present. To raise that WUML just a little further, try …

**Minute Three:** Brush Your Teeth

As soon as you've gotten out of bed and turned off your alarm clock, go directly to the bathroom sink to brush your teeth. I know what you may be thinking: *Really? You're telling me that I need to brush my teeth?* Yes. The point is that you're doing mindless activities for the first few minutes and simply giving your body time to wake up.

After turning off your alarm clock, go directly to the bathroom sink, brush your teeth, and splash some warm (or cold) water on your face. This simple activity will allow for the passing of more time to increase your WUML even further.

Now that your mouth is minty fresh, it's time to…

**Minute Four:** Drink a Full Glass of Water

It's crucial that you hydrate yourself first thing every morning. After six to eight hours without water, you'll be mildly dehydrated, which causes fatigue. Often when people feel tired—at any time of the day—what they really need is more water, not more sleep.

Start by getting a glass or bottle of water (or do what we do— fill it up the night before so it's already there for you in the morning), and drink it as fast as is comfortable for you. The objective is to replace the water you were deprived of during the hours you slept. (And hey, the side benefits of morning hydration include better, younger-looking skin and healthy weight maintenance. Not bad for a few ounces of water!)

That glass of water should raise your WUML another notch, which will get you to …

**Minute Five:** Get Dressed in Your Workout Clothes (or Jump in the Shower)

The fifth step has two options.

*Option one* is to get dressed in your exercise clothing so you're ready to leave your bedroom and immediately engage in your Miracle Morning. You can lay out your clothes before you go to bed or even sleep in your workout clothes (yes, really). For teachers, the "night before" prep is especially important to help you go straight into your practice. If you have kids, you can make this part of their bedtime ritual so they build the habit too.

*Option two* is to jump in the shower, which is a great way to take your WUML to the point where staying awake is much easier. However, I usually opt to change into exercise clothes, since I'll need a shower after working out, and I believe there is something to be said about *earning* your morning shower! But a lot of people prefer the morning shower because it helps them wake up and gives them a fresh start to the day. The choice is completely yours.

Regardless of which option you choose, by the time you've executed these five simple steps, your WUML should be high enough that it requires very little discipline to stay awake for your Miracle Morning.

If you tried to make that commitment the moment your alarm clock first went off—while you were at a WUML of nearly zero—it would be a much more difficult decision to make. The five steps let you build momentum so that, within just a few minutes, you're ready to go instead of feeling groggy.

I have never made it through the first five minutes and decided to go back to bed. Once I am up and moving intentionally through the morning, being purposeful throughout the day is much easier.

## Miracle Morning Bonus Wake-Up Tips

Although this strategy has worked for thousands of people, these five steps are not the only way to make waking up in the morning easier. Here are a few others I've heard from fellow Miracle Morning practitioners:

- *The Miracle Morning Bedtime Affirmations*: If you haven't done so yet, take a moment now to go to www.TMMBook.com and download the re-energizing, intention-setting *Bedtime Affirmations* for free. Nothing is more effective for ensuring that you will wake up before your alarm than programming your mind to achieve exactly what you want.

- Set a timer for your bedroom lights: One member of The Miracle Morning Community shared that he sets his bedroom lights on a timer (you can buy an appliance timer online or at your local hardware store). As his alarm goes off, the lights come on in the room. What a great idea! It's a lot easier to fall back asleep when it's dark; having the lights on tells your mind and body that it's time to wake up. (Whether you use a timer or not, be sure to turn your light on right after you turn your alarm off.)

- Set a timer for your bedroom heater: Another member of The Miracle Morning Community says that in the winter, she keeps a bedroom heater on an appliance timer set to go off fifteen minutes before she wakes up. She keeps it cold at night but warm for waking up so she won't be tempted to crawl back under her covers.

Feel free to add to or customize the Five-Minute Snooze-Proof Wake-Up Strategy, and if you have any tips that you're open to sharing, we'd love to hear them. Please post them in The Miracle Morning Community at www.MyTMMCommunity.com.

Waking up consistently and easily is all about having an effective, predetermined, step-by-step strategy to increase your WUML in the morning. Don't wait to try this! Start tonight by reading *The Miracle Morning Bedtime Affirmations* to set a powerful intention for waking up tomorrow morning, move your alarm clock across the room, set a glass of water on your nightstand or bathroom counter, and commit to the other two steps for the morning.

## Taking Immediate Action

There's no need to wait to get started implementing the power of early rising. As Anthony Robbins has said, "When is NOW a good time for you to do that?" Now, indeed, would be perfect! In fact, the sooner you start, the sooner you'll begin to see results, including increased energy, a better attitude, and, of course, a happier classroom.

**Step One:** Set your alarm for thirty to sixty minutes earlier than you usually wake up, for the next thirty days. That's it; just thirty to sixty minutes for thirty days, starting now. And be sure to write into your schedule to do your first Miracle Morning...*tomorrow morning*. That's right, don't use *waiting until you finish the book* as an excuse to procrastinate on getting started!

If you feel resistant at all, it may be because you've tried to make changes in the past but haven't followed through. If you haven't already, go ahead and turn now to "Chapter 10: The Miracle Morning 30-Day Transformation Challenge" and get started right now on your first 30-Day Challenge. This will not only give you the mindset and strategy to overcome any resistance you may have to getting started, but it will give you the most effective process for implementing and sticking with a new habit. Think of it as beginning with the end in mind.

From this day forward, starting with the next thirty days, keep your alarm set for thirty to sixty minutes earlier than the time that you *have* to wake up so that you can start waking up when you *want* to, instead of when you *have* to. It's time to start launching each day with a Miracle Morning so that you can become the person you need to be to lead yourself, your family, and your students to extraordinary levels of success and fulfillment.

What will you do with that hour? You're going to find out in the next chapter, but for now, simply continue reading this book during your Miracle Morning until you learn the whole routine.

**Step Two:** You may have already taken this step, but in case you haven't, we invite you to join either The Miracle Morning Community at MyTMMCommunity.com or The Miracle Morning for Teachers Community at TMMTeacherCommunity.com (or both!) to connect with and get support from other like-minded early risers, many of whom have been practicing the Miracle Morning for years.

**Step Three:** Find your Miracle Morning accountability partner. Enroll someone—a fellow teacher, your spouse, a friend, a family member, or someone you meet in one of the Miracle Morning

Communities—to join you on this adventure so you can encourage, support, and hold each other accountable to follow through until your Miracle Morning has become a lifelong habit.

Okay, now let's get into the six most powerful, proven personal development practices known to man (or woman)...the Life S.A.V.E.R.S.

## Meet Legendary Teacher-Contributor
# Allison Dillard
### Math professor, speaker, and author of *Crush Math Now* and *Raise Your Math Grade*

I teach Pre-Algebra— the lowest-level math a student can place into—at a community college. My students have low confidence, high anxiety, and weak foundations in math. On our first day, I wrote S.A.V.E.R.S. on the board, explained how the Miracle Morning had helped me and how each practice could benefit math students. We started every class for a month with six minutes of S.A.V.E.R.S.

During **Silence**, I asked the class to sit up straight, close their eyes, and breathe deeply. I asked them to let go of their insecurities and focus on challenges I presented. As the month progressed, I gave them freedom to experiment. Some continued the breathing exercise. Others meditated. Still others prayed.

Students wrote down their math goals as **Affirmations**. Was it a passing grade? Or an A on the next quiz? Each class, they wrote more, like why their goals were important to them or how they were achieving them. They also revised goals to make them bigger or more specific.

For **Visualization**, I put a math problem on the board and the students visualized the steps to order of operations problems. I discovered this to be an effective way to strengthen their math foundations.

We experimented with **Exercises**, trying everything from jump squats, which they hated, to stretching, which they loved.

For **Reading**, I gave the class a passage to read. The passages varied from math test-taking tips, to an article on Kobe Bryant discussing failure, to the results of experiments on test anxiety. The few times I chose a passage that wasn't interesting, it felt like a wasted minute. However, when the passage was motivating or informative, the minute of reading was powerful.

**Scribing** varied from class to class. Students wrote about the passage they just read. They wrote about their math fears and brainstormed solutions. They added to or edited the goals they set for their Affirmations. Each writing exercise was helpful in different ways.

The results of our month of the Miracle Morning surprised me. The class's attendance and homework completion rates rose to over 90 percent, the highest they've ever been for my Pre-Algebra class. The scores on their quizzes were phenomenal, even though I went out of my way to give them hard quizzes. Anxious students found that meditating on and writing about their anxiety assuaged their fears. Students who lacked motivation and discipline said writing and reading their Affirmations helped them attend class more often and complete more homework. Many students found visualization helped them study for quizzes.

I absolutely love the Miracle Morning. It has helped me turn a boring math requirement that students take only because they have no choice into something that will positively affect the rest of their lives.

## Meet Legendary Teacher-Contributor
# Ashley Weisz
### Acton Academy West Elementary School, Austin, Texas

I knew the Miracle Morning was something special after finishing college. In my first year of teaching on my own, I needed something to ground me. During that first year, my Google searches included:

Elementary / Pre-K classroom management

How to not cry in your car during your first year of teaching (Hint: I cried daily that first year. I think we all do.)

As we all know, all online activity is connected, and somehow, from my Google searches, *The Miracle Morning* came up on my Pinterest on the "Things You Might Like" board. I clicked the link and was forever changed. My mornings became my sacred hours, forming me into a stronger, more confident teacher. When the opportunity arose to introduce TMM to my class, I was more than willing and excited. After our first visualization, I knew they felt what I felt after my first TMM experience.

Our first morning felt a little awkward. There was a lot of shifting, one-eye-open classroom scanning, and circle drawing instead of scribing. But in the classroom during core skills, we saw changes immediately. We chose S.A.V.S.E.R. instead of S.A.V.E.R.S. I feel that reading is such a personal, individual activity that it should be done anywhere they feel comfortable: resting in bean bags, lounging under desks, sitting on top of desks, sprawled on carpets or hardwood floors, or leaning against bookshelves. This order worked perfectly for us, and on the mornings we started our day with TMM, we were twice as productive as before we were starting our days intentionally. Our students agree!

*"I loved how M.M. woke me up! I am not a huge morning person, and this helped me become one. The visualization was my favorite because it showed me how I WOULD have a good day, and I did have a good day every time!"*—Cameron

*"I'm changed at school because of Miracle Morning. Every day when we do the visualization, say I chose "I AM POSITIVE," that day I am super positive! For example, if I'm playing basketball and I miss a shot, I now say, 'That was so close!' instead of, 'What!? That should have gone in...come on!!'"*—Slaton

*"It really helps clear your mind, and it makes you feel calm. It sends your body into a whole new place and sends your mind to a successful road instead of a dark road."*—Clara

*"Think about yourself as a flower. You have to start blossoming soon, but you don't know how. You need water, sun and lots of love from others, but it is your job to start blossoming. But then, there is a gardener who gives you lots of love, water, and sunshine. This is why you can't do EVERYTHING by yourself. You need the love from others, and during Miracle Morning, you can visualize that."*—Sophie E.

We changed as a community after our time together. Our students ask for it daily, and we have decided as a school to incorporate it into our permanent schedule.

# — 3 —
# THE LIFE S.A.V.E.R.S

## SIX PRACTICES GUARANTEED TO SAVE YOU FROM A LIFE OF UNFULFILLED POTENTIAL

*What Hal has done with his acronym S.A.V.E.R.S. is take the best practices—developed over centuries of human consciousness development—and condensed the "best of the best" into a daily morning ritual. A ritual that is now part of my day. Many people do one of the S.A.V.E.R.S. daily. For example, many people do the **E**, they exercise every morning. Others do **S** for silence or meditation, or **S** for scribing or journaling. But until Hal packaged S.A.V.E.R.S., no one was doing all six ancient "best practices" every morning. Going through S.A.V.E.R.S. every morning is like pumping rocket fuel into my body, mind, and spirit ... before I start my day, every day.*

—ROBERT KIYOSAKI, BESTSELLING AUTHOR OF
*RICH DAD POOR DAD*

Most people live their lives on the wrong side of a significant gap that separates who we are from who we can become, which holds us back from creating the life we truly want. Often frustrated with ourselves—and our lack of consistent motivation, effort, and results in one or more areas of life—we spend too much time *thinking* about the actions we should be taking to create the results that we want, but then we don't take those actions. More often than not, we know what we need to do…we just don't consistently *do* it.

Do you ever feel like that? As if the life you want—and the person and teacher you know you need to be in order to create it—is just beyond your grasp? When you see other teachers who are excelling in an area, or playing at a level that you're not, does it ever seem like they've got it all figured out? Like they must know something that you don't know, because if you knew it, then you'd be excelling too?

When Hal experienced the second of his two rock bottoms (the first was when he died for six minutes in a car crash, and the second was when he experienced financial ruin during the economic crash of 2008), he felt lost and depressed. Applying what he already knew wasn't working. Nothing he tried was improving his situation. So he began his own quest for the fastest, most effective strategy to turn his life around and take his success to the next level. He went in search of the best personal development practices, those things that the world's most successful people practiced in all walks of life.

After discovering and assembling a list of six of the most timeless, effective, and proven personal development practices in history, he first attempted to determine which one or two would accelerate his success the fastest. However, his breakthrough occurred when he asked himself, *what would happen if I did ALL of these?*

So, he did. Within just two months of implementing all six practices, nearly every single day, Hal experienced what you might call "miraculous" results. He overcame his depression, more than doubled his income, and immediately began training to run a 52-mile ultramarathon—ironically, because he was *not* a runner. In fact, he despised running and had never run more than one mile. However, his new mindset was that by committing to run fifty-two consecutive miles in a single day, he would have to develop his physical, mental, and emotional abilities to levels beyond what he had ever experienced before. In other words, he made a decision to dedicate time each day to practice the S.A.V.E.R.S. in order to become the level ten person he needed to be to create the level ten life that he had always wanted.

Whether you're already very successful, like self-made multimillionaire Robert Kiyosaki (who practices the Miracle Morning and the S.A.V.E.R.S. nearly every single day), or if you've ever felt like the life you want to live—and the person you know you can be—are just beyond your grasp, the Life S.A.V.E.R.S. are virtually guaranteed to save you from missing out on the extraordinary life that you truly want and deserve to live.

## Why the Life S.A.V.E.R.S. Work

The Life S.A.V.E.R.S. (or SAVERS for short) are simple, but profoundly effective, daily morning practices that are virtually guaranteed to enable you to become more so that you can fulfill your potential. They give you space to gain heightened levels of clarity and to plan and live your life on your terms. They're designed to start your day by putting you in a peak physical, mental, emotional, and spiritual state so that you continually improve, feel great, and always perform at your best.

I know, I know. You don't have time. Before starting the Miracle Morning, I would wake up to pure chaos, with barely enough time to get myself dressed, fed, and out the door for the first activity of the day. You probably think you can hardly squeeze in what you *have* to do already, never mind what you *want* to do. But I "didn't have time" before the Miracle Morning either. And yet, here I am now with more time, more prosperity, and a more peaceful life than I've ever had before.

What you need to realize right now is that your Miracle Morning will create time for you. The Life S.A.V.E.R.S. are the vehicle to help you reconnect with your true essence and wake up with purpose instead of obligation. The practices help you build energy, see priorities more clearly, and find the most productive flow in your life.

In other words, the S.A.V.E.R.S. don't *take* time from your day but ultimately *add* more to it.

Each letter in S.A.V.E.R.S. represents one of the best practices of the most successful people on the planet. From A-list movie stars and world-class professional athletes to CEOs and entrepreneurs, you'd be hard-pressed to find an elite performer who didn't swear by at least one of the S.A.V.E.R.S.

However, you'd be equally hard-pressed to find an elite performer who practices even half, let alone ALL of the S.A.V.E.R.S. (well, I guess that's changing now that Hal has introduced the world to the Miracle Morning). That's what makes the Miracle Morning so effective—you're harnessing the game-changing benefits of not just one but all six of *the best practices, developed over centuries of human consciousness development,* and combining them all into a concise, fully customizable morning ritual.

The S.A.V.E.R.S. are:

**Si**lence

**A**ffirmations

**V**isualization

**E**xercise

**R**eading

**S**cribing

Leveraging these six practices is how you will accelerate your personal development by maximizing the impact of your newfound Miracle Morning ritual. They're customizable to fit you, your lifestyle, your business, and your specific goals. And you can start implementing them first thing tomorrow morning.

Let's go through each of the S.A.V.E.R.S. in detail.

# S is for Silence

Silence, the first practice of the S.A.V.E.R.S., is a key habit for teachers. If you've been guilty of starting your day by immediately grabbing your phone or computer and diving into emails, phone calls, social media, and text messages, then this is your opportunity to learn the power of beginning each day with peaceful, purposeful *silence.*

Like I did before the Miracle Morning, most people start the day when their alarm signifies they *must* get up. And most people run from morning to night, struggling to regain control for the rest of the day. It's not a coincidence. Starting each day with a period of silence instead will immediately reduce your stress levels and help you begin the day with the kind of calm and clarity that you need in order to focus on what's most important.

Remember, many of the world's most successful people are daily practitioners of silence. That shows you how important it is. It's not surprising that Oprah practices stillness—or that she does nearly all of the other S.A.V.E.R.S. too. Musician Katy Perry practices transcendental meditation, as do Sheryl Crow and Sir Paul McCartney. Film and television stars Jennifer Aniston, Ellen DeGeneres, Jerry Seinfeld, Howard Stern, Cameron Diaz, Clint Eastwood, and Hugh Jackman have all spoken of their daily meditation practice. Hip hop mogul Russell Simmons meditates with his two daughters every morning for twenty minutes. Even famous billionaires Ray Dalio and Rupert Murdoch have attributed their financial success to the daily practice of stillness. You'll be in good (and quiet) company by doing the same.

If it seems like I'm asking you to do nothing, let me clarify: you have many choices for your practice of silence. In no particular order, here are a few to get you started:

- Meditation
- Prayer
- Reflection
- Deep breathing
- Gratitude

Whichever you choose, be sure you don't stay in bed for your period of silence, and better still, get out of your bedroom altogether.

In an interview with *Shape* magazine, actress and singer Kristen Bell said, "Do meditative yoga for 10 minutes every morning. When you have a problem—whether it's road rage, your guy, or work—meditation allows everything to unfold the way it's supposed to."

And don't be afraid to expand your horizons. Meditation comes in many forms. As Angelina Jolie told *Stylist* magazine, "I find meditation in sitting on the floor with the kids coloring for an hour, or going on the trampoline. You do what you love, that makes you happy, and that gives you your meditation."

## The Benefits of Silence

How many times do we find ourselves in stressful situations? How many times do we deal with immediate needs that take us away from our vision or plan? Stress is one of the most common side effects of teaching. We face the ever-present distractions of other people encroaching on our schedule and the inevitable fires we must extinguish. Your fellow teachers (and, of course, your students) have the uncanny ability to push your stress buttons. The student who forgets their homework or has a stressful home issue that needs to be dealt with can take priority over what you're there to do: teach. Not to mention administrative tasks (and the administration!) that need to be handled.

Excessive stress is terrible for your health. It triggers your fight-or-flight response, and that releases a cascade of toxic hormones that can stay in your body for days. That's fine if you experience that type of stress only occasionally. Teaching, however, can be an everyday stressor, which is why practicing regular meditation can come in handy.

According to PsychologyToday.com, "The stress hormone, cortisol, is public health enemy number one. Scientists have known for years that elevated cortisol levels: interfere with learning and memory, lower immune function and bone density, increase weight gain, blood pressure, cholesterol, heart disease... The list goes on and on. Chronic stress and elevated cortisol levels also increase risk for depression, mental illness, and lower life expectancy."

Silence in the form of meditation reduces stress and, as a result, improves your health. A major study run by several groups, including the National Institutes of Health, the American Medical Association, the Mayo Clinic, and scientists from both Harvard and Stanford, revealed that meditation reduces stress and high blood pressure. A recent study by Dr. Norman Rosenthal, a world-renowned psychiatrist who works with the David Lynch Foundation, even found that people who practice meditation are 30 percent less likely to die from heart disease.

Another study from Harvard found that just eight weeks of meditation could lead to "increased gray-matter density in the hippocampus, known to be important for learning and memory, and in structures associated with self-awareness, compassion, and introspection."

Meditation helps you to slow down and focus on you, even if it's for just a short time.

"I started meditating because I felt like I needed stop my life from running me," singer Sheryl Crow has said. "Meditation helped slow my day down." She continues to devote twenty minutes in the morning and twenty minutes at night to meditation.

Monica Dix, a mom in The Miracle Morning Community, shared the following story. At breakfast, her five-year-old daughter told her, "I like when you pretend you're on top of a mountain." Monica asked her what she meant, and she responded, "When you're pretending that you're on a mountain and the sky is clear and you're just breathing." Monica asked, "Do you mean when I am meditating?" Her daughter replied, "Yes!" She paused, then added, "I wish you would do it more, you're being a good mama." It's so encouraging when our children see the effort we are putting in for their benefit and cheer us on!

Being silent opens a space for you to secure your own oxygen mask before assisting others. The benefits are extraordinary and can bring you much-needed clarity and peace of mind. Practicing silence, in other words, can help you reduce your stress, improve cognitive performance, and become confident at the same time.

## Guided Meditations and Meditation Apps

Meditation is like anything else—if you've never done it before, then it can be difficult or feel awkward at first. If you are a first-time meditator, a great place to start is with a guided meditation.

Here are a few meditation apps that are available for both iPhone/iPad and Android devices:

- Headspace
- Calm
- Omvana
- Simply Being
- Insight Timer

There are subtle and significant differences among these meditation apps, one of which is the voice of the person speaking.

If you don't have a device that allows you to download apps, simply go to YouTube or Google and search for the keywords "guided meditation." You can also search by duration (i.e. "five-minute guided meditation") or topic (i.e. "guided meditation for increased confidence").

## Miracle Morning (Individual) Meditation

When you're ready to try meditating on your own, here is a simple, step-by-step meditation you can use during your Miracle Morning, even if you've never done this before.

- Before beginning, it's important to prepare yourself and set expectations. This is a time for you to quiet your mind and let go of the compulsive need to constantly be thinking about something—reliving the past or worrying about the future, but never living fully in the present. This is the time to let go of your stresses, take a break from worrying about your problems, and be here in this moment. It is a time to access the essence of who you truly are—to go deeper than what you have, what you do, or the labels you've accepted as who you are. If this sounds foreign to you, or too New Age-y, that's okay. I've felt the same way. It's probably because you've never tried it before. But thankfully, you're about to.

• Find a quiet, comfortable place to sit. You can sit on the couch, on a chair, on the floor, or on a pillow for added comfort.

• Sit upright, cross-legged. You can close your eyes, or you can look down at a point on the ground about two feet in front of you.

• Begin by focusing on your breath, taking slow, deep breaths. Breathe in through the nose and out through the mouth. The most effective breathing causes your belly to expand and not your chest.

• Now start pacing your breath; breathe in slowly for a count of three seconds (one one thousand, two one thousand, three one thousand), hold it in for another three counts, and then breathe out slowly for a final count of three. Feel your thoughts and emotions settling down as you focus on your breath. Be aware that, as you attempt to quiet your mind, thoughts will still come in to pay a visit. Simply acknowledge them and then let them go, always returning your focus to your breath.

• Allow yourself to be fully present in this moment. This is often referred to as "being." Not thinking, not doing, just being. Continue to follow your breath, and imagine inhaling positive, loving, and peaceful energy and exhaling all your worries and stress. Enjoy the quiet. Enjoy the moment. Just breathe … Just be.

• If you find that you have a constant influx of thoughts, it may be helpful for you to focus on a single word, phrase, or mantra and repeat it over and over again to yourself as you inhale and exhale. For example, you might try something like this: (On the inhale) "I inhale confidence …" (As you exhale) "I exhale fear …" You can swap the word "confidence" for whatever you feel you need to bring more of into your life (love, faith, energy, etc.), and swap the word "fear" with whatever you feel you need to let go of (stress, worry, resentment, etc.).

• Meditation is a gift you can give yourself every day. My time spent meditating has become one of my favorite parts of the Miracle Morning routine. It's a time to be at peace and to experience gratitude and freedom from my day-to-day stressors and worries.

Think of daily meditation as a temporary vacation from your problems. Although your problems will still be there when you finish your daily meditation, you'll find that you're more centered and better equipped to handle or solve them.

## A is for Affirmations

Have you ever wondered how some people seem to just be good at *everything* they do and consistently achieve at a level so high, you can hardly comprehend how you're ever going to join them? Or why others seem to drop every ball? Time and time again, it is a person's *mindset* that has proven to be the driving factor in their results.

Mindset can be defined as the accumulation of beliefs, attitude, and emotional intelligence. In her bestselling book, *Mindset: The New Psychology of Success*, Carol Dweck, Ph.D., states: "For twenty years, my research has shown that the view you adopt of yourself profoundly affects the way you lead your life."

Others can easily sense your mindset. It shows up undeniably in your language, your confidence, and your demeanor. Your mindset affects everything! Show me someone with a successful mindset, and I'll show you a successful educator!

I know firsthand, though, how difficult it can be to maintain the right mindset—the confidence, enthusiasm, not to mention motivation—during the roller coaster ride that comes with being a teacher. Mindset is largely something we adopt without conscious thought; at a subconscious level, we have been programmed to think, believe, act, and talk to ourselves a certain way.

Our programming comes from many influences, including what others have told us, what we tell ourselves, and all of our good and bad life experiences. That programming expresses itself in every area of our lives, including the way we behave around our students. And that means if we want a better classroom dynamic, we need better mental programming.

Affirmations are a tool for doing just that. They enable you to become more intentional about your goals while also providing the encouragement and positive mindset necessary to achieve them. When you repeatedly tell yourself who you want to be, what you want to accomplish, and how you are going to achieve it, your subconscious mind will shift your beliefs and behavior. Once you believe and act in new ways, you will begin to manifest your affirmations into reality.

Science has proven that affirmations—when done correctly—are one of the most effective tools for quickly becoming the person you need to be to achieve everything you want—for yourself and your life and your classroom. And yet, affirmations also get a bad rap. Many people have tried them only to be disappointed with little or no results. However, there is a way to leverage affirmations in a way that will absolutely produce results for you.

By repeatedly articulating and reinforcing to yourself **what** result you want to accomplish, **why** accomplishing it is important to you, **which** specific actions are required to produce that result, and, most importantly, precisely **when** you will commit to taking those actions, your subconscious mind will shift your beliefs and behavior. You'll begin to automatically believe and act in new ways, and eventually manifest your affirmations into your reality. But first...

# Why the Old Way of Doing Affirmations Does Not Work

For decades, countless so-called experts and gurus have taught affirmations in ways that have proven to be ineffective and set people up for failure. Here are two of the most common problems with affirmations.

## Problem #1: Lying to Yourself Doesn't Work

*I am a millionaire.* Really?

*I have 7 percent body fat.* Do you?

*I have achieved all of my goals this year.* Have you?

Creating affirmations as if you've already become or achieved something that you have yet to become or achieve may be the single biggest obstacle to affirmations being effective, for most people.

With this technique, every time you recite the affirmation that isn't rooted in truth, your subconscious will resist it. As an intelligent human being who isn't delusional, lying to yourself repeatedly will never be the optimum strategy. *The truth will always prevail.*

## Problem #2: Passive Language Doesn't Produce Results

Many affirmations have been designed to make you feel good by creating an empty promise of something you desire. For example, here is a popular money affirmation that's been perpetuated by many world-famous gurus:

*I am a money magnet. Money flows to me effortlessly and in abundance.*

This type of affirmation might make you feel good in the moment by giving you a false sense of relief from your financial worries, but it won't generate any income. People who sit back and wait for money to show up magically are cash poor.

To generate the kind of abundance you want (or any result you desire, for that matter), you've got to actually do something. Your actions must be in alignment with your desired results, and your affirmations must articulate and affirm both.

# Four Steps to Create Miracle Morning Affirmations (That Produce Results)

Here are simple steps to create and implement results-oriented Miracle Morning affirmations that will program your conscious and subconscious mind, while redirecting your conscious mind to upgrade your behavior so that you can begin to produce results and take your levels of personal and professional success beyond what you've ever experienced before.

## Step One: Identify The Ideal Result You Are Committed to and Why

Notice I'm not starting with what you *want*. Everyone wants things, but we don't get what we want; we get what we're committed to. You want to be a great role model for your students? Who doesn't? Join that nonexclusive club. Oh wait, you're 100 percent committed to becoming "Teacher of the Year" by clarifying and executing the necessary actions until the result is achieved? Okay, now we're talking.

**Action:** Start by writing down a specific, extraordinary result or outcome—one that challenges you, would significantly improve your life, and that you are ready to commit to creating—even if you're not yet sure how you will do it. Then reinforce your commitment by including your *why*: the compelling reason you're willing to stay committed.

**Examples:** *I am dedicated to encouraging and helping each of my students to get the best grades they can possibly get.*

Or …

*I am 100 percent committed to being the best person I can be so that I can be the best teacher I can be, one that is fully present with my students and fellow teachers.*

Or ...

*I am committed to increasing my students' test scores during this next school year, from _____ to _____, so that my students can achieve whatever they want in life.*

## Step Two: Decide The Necessary Actions You Are Committed to Taking and *When*

Writing an affirmation that merely affirms what you *want* without affirming what you are committed to *doing* is one step above pointless and can be counterproductive by tricking your subconscious mind into thinking that the result will happen automatically, without effort.

**Action:** Clarify the (specific) action, activity, or habit that is required for you to achieve your ideal outcome, and clearly state when and how often you will execute the necessary action.

**Examples:** *To help my students get into a peak physical, mental, and emotional state, I am committed to leading them through the Life S.A.V.E.R.S. at the start of each school day.*

Or ...

*To ensure that I am the best teacher I can be, I am 100 percent committed to doing my Miracle Morning each day from 6:00 a.m. to 7:00 a.m.*

Or ...

*To guarantee that my students increase their test scores, I am committed to tutoring my students one on one before school, from 7:15-7:30 a.m., and doing the Life S.A.V.E.R.S. five days a week from 8:00 a.m. to 8:06 a.m.—NO MATTER WHAT.*

The more specific your actions are, the better. The more effectively you articulate and solidify your commitment to those actions, the more likely you are to follow through with them. Be sure to include *frequency* (how often), *quantity* (how many), and *precise time frames* (when you will begin and end your activities).

## Step Three: Recite Your Affirmations Every Morning (with Emotion)

Remember, your Miracle Morning affirmations aren't designed merely to make you *feel good*. These written statements are strategically engineered to program your subconscious mind with the beliefs and mindset you need to achieve your desired outcomes while directing your conscious mind to keep you focused on your highest priorities and the actions that will get you there.

For your affirmations to be effective, however, it is important that you tap into your emotions while reciting them. Mindlessly repeating an affirmation without intentionally feeling its truth will have minimal impact for you. You must take responsibility for generating authentic emotions, such as excitement and determination, and powerfully infusing those emotions into every affirmation you recite.

You must affirm who you need to be to do the things you need to do so that you can have the results that you want. I'll say this again: it isn't magic; this strategy works when you connect with *the person you need to become* on the way to achieving your goals. It's who you are that attracts your results more than any other activity.

**Action:** Schedule time each day to read your affirmations during your Miracle Morning to both program your subconscious and focus your conscious mind on what's most important to you and what you are committed to doing to make it your reality. That's right, you must read them daily. Reading your affirmations occasionally is as effective as an occasional workout. You'll start seeing results only when you've made them a part of your daily routine.

A great place to read affirmations is in the shower. If you laminate them and leave them there, then they will be in front of you every day. Put them anywhere you will see them often: under your car's sun visor, taped to your mirror. The more you see them, the more the subconscious mind can connect with them to change your thinking and your actions. You can even write them directly on a mirror with dry erase markers or shower crayons.

## Step Four: Constantly Update and Evolve Your Affirmations

As you continue to grow, improve, and evolve, so should your affirmations. When you come up with a new goal, dream, or any extraordinary result you want to create for your life, add it to your affirmations.

Personally, I have affirmations for every single significant area of my life (finances, health, happiness, relationships, parenting, etc.), and I continually update them as I learn more. And I am always on the lookout for quotes, strategies, and philosophies that I can add to improve my mindset. Any time you come across an empowering quote or philosophy and think to yourself, *Wow, that is an area where I could make a huge improvement*, add it to your affirmations.

Remember, your affirmations should be tailored to you, and phrased in the form of "I" statements. They must be specific for them to work in your subconscious.

Your programming can change and improve at any time, starting right now. You can reprogram any perceived limitations with new beliefs and create new behaviors so you can become as successful as you want to be in any area of life you choose.

In summary, your new affirmations articulate the extraordinary results you are committed to creating, why they are critically important to you, and, most importantly, which necessary actions you are committed to taking and when to ensure that you attain and sustain the extraordinary levels of success you truly want (and deserve) for your life.

## Affirmations to Become a Legendary Teacher

In addition to the formula to create your affirmations, I have included this list of sample affirmations, which may help spark your creativity. Feel free to include any of these that resonate with you.

- I am just as worthy, deserving, and capable of being an incredible teacher as any other person on earth, and I will prove that today with my actions.
- Where I am is a result of who I *was*, but where I go depends entirely on who I *choose to be*, starting today.
- I am fully committed to dedicating thirty to sixty minutes to do my Miracle Morning and the S.A.V.E.R.S. so that I can continue to become the person I need to be to create everything I want for my life.
- I am fully committed to being the best teacher I can be, because I know that who I'm being will positively impact my students' lives, and I want them to have the best start in life.
- I focus on learning new things and improving my teaching skills daily, and I commit to reading or rereading at least one new book to help that effort every month.
- I am committed to constant and never-ending improvement in the tasks necessary for my optimal day-to-day functioning.
- I commit to putting myself in a peak state every day before I see even one student or other faculty member so I can make the most positive impact possible on everyone with whom I come in contact.
- I am committed to my personal growth and reading for twenty minutes every day.

These are just a few examples of affirmations. You can use any that resonate with you, but do create your own using the four-step formula described in the previous pages. Anything you say repeatedly to yourself, with emotion, will be programmed into your subconscious mind, help you form new beliefs, and manifest itself through your actions.

# V is for Visualization

Visualization has long been a well-known practice of world-class athletes who use it to optimize their performance. Olympic athletes and top performers in many categories incorporate visualization as a critical part of their daily training. What is less well-known is that successful people everywhere, the true top achievers in any field (yes, including teaching), use it just as frequently.

Visualization is a technique in which you use your imagination to create a compelling picture of your future, providing you with heightened clarity and producing the motivation that will assist you in making your vision a reality.

If you'd like some fascinating information about *why* visualization works, just Google "mirror neurons." A neuron is a cell that connects the brain and other parts of the body; a mirror neuron fires when we take an action or observe someone else taking an action. This is a relatively new area of study in neurology, but these cells seem to allow us to improve our abilities by watching other people perform them *or* by visualizing ourselves performing them. Some studies indicate that experienced weightlifters can increase muscle mass through vivid visualization sessions, and mirror neurons get the credit for making this possible. In many ways, the brain can't tell the difference between a vivid visualization and an actual experience. Crazy, right?

I was always a little skeptical about the value of visualization because it sounded a little too New Age-y. Once I read about mirror neurons, my whole attitude changed! You can't argue with science, right?

## What do You Visualize?

Most anyone is limited by visions of their past results, replaying previous failures and heartbreaks. Creative visualization, on the other hand, enables you to design the vision that will occupy your mind, ensuring that the greatest pull on you is your future—a compelling, exciting, and limitless future.

After I've read my affirmations, I sit upright, close my eyes, and take a few slow, deep breaths. For the next five to ten minutes, I simply visualize the *specific actions* that are necessary for my long- and short-term goals to become a reality.

Notice that I did *not* say that I visualize the results. Many people will disagree on this, but there are studies that provide scientific evidence showing that merely visualizing the result you want (e.g. the new car, the dream house, crossing the finish line, standing on stage, etc.) can diminish your drive because your brain has already experienced the reward on some level. Instead, I highly recommend focusing your visualization on the necessary actions, more so than the results. Visualize yourself taking the actions—especially the actions that you habitually resist and procrastinate on—in a way that creates a compelling mental and emotional experience of the action. For example, Hal despised running, but he had made a commitment to himself (and publicly) to run a 52-mile ultra-marathon. Throughout the course of his five months of training, he used Miracle Morning Visualization to see himself lacing up his running shoes and hitting the pavement—*with a smile on his face and pep in his step*—so that when it was time to train, he had already programmed the experience to be positive and enjoyable.

You might picture yourself having fun and light conversations with your students. Or, you might spend time imagining your students all getting 100 percent test scores. What does your picture of success look like? How do you feel as you watch students checking their papers for their score, seeing the smiles on their faces as they realize they got the A+ they've been visualizing and working toward?

Picture yourself responding to any obstacles and issues—such as miscalculations, misspellings, or even missed deadlines—calmly. See yourself encouraging your students to do better next time or giving them a high five when they realize "they did it." You can see yourself staying calm when a student is unruly or disrespectful and handling challenging situations with ease and grace. And be sure to see yourself celebrating and feeling fantastic when things go better than planned!

You can pick anything that is a critical action step or skill that you may not be performing at your best yet. Envisioning success and what it takes to get there will prepare you for, and almost ensure, a successful day.

# Three Simple Steps for Miracle Morning Visualization

The perfect time to visualize yourself living in alignment with your affirmations is right after you read them.

## Step One: Get Ready

Some people like to play instrumental music in the background during their visualization, such as classical or baroque (check out anything from the composer J. S. Bach). If you'd like to experiment with music, put it on with the volume relatively low. Personally, I find anything with words to be a distraction.

Now, sit up tall in a comfortable position. This can be on a chair, the couch, or a cushion on the floor. Breathe deeply. Close your eyes, clear your mind, and let go of any self-imposed limitations as you prepare yourself for the benefits of visualization.

## Step Two: Visualize What You Really Want

Many people don't feel comfortable visualizing success and are even scared to succeed. Some people may experience resistance in this area. Some may even feel guilty that they will leave the other 95 percent behind when they become successful.

This famous quote from Marianne Williamson is a great reminder for anyone who feels mental or emotional obstacles when attempting to visualize: "Our deepest fear is not that we are inadequate. Our deepest fear is that we are powerful beyond measure. It is our light, not our darkness that most frightens us. We ask ourselves, 'Who am I to be brilliant, gorgeous, talented, fabulous?' Actually, who are you not to be? You are a child of God. Your playing small does not serve the world. There is nothing enlightened about shrinking so that other people won't feel insecure around you. We are all meant to shine, as children do. We were born to make manifest the glory of God that is within us. It's not just in some of us; it's in everyone. And as we let our own light shine, we unconsciously give other people permission to do the same. As we are liberated from our own fear, our presence automatically liberates others."

Consider that the greatest gift you can give to those you love—and those you teach—is to live to your full potential. What does that look like for you? What do you really want? Forget about logic, limits, and practicality. If you could reach any heights, personally and professionally, what would that look like?

See, feel, hear, touch, taste, and smell every detail of your vision. Involve all your senses to maximize effectiveness. The more vivid you make your vision, the more compelled you'll be to take the necessary actions to make it a reality (and the faster it will become your reality!).

## Step Three: Visualize Yourself Taking (and Enjoying) the Necessary Actions

Once you've created a clear mental picture of what you want, begin to see yourself doing precisely what you need to do to achieve your vision, with supreme confidence and while enjoying every step of the process. See yourself engaged in the actions you'll need to take (exercising, writing, teaching, giving tests and exams, grading papers, working one on one with students, meeting with parents, taking continuing education classes, etc.). Picture yourself with a look and *feeling* of supreme confidence as you are delivering your lessons and seeing the recognition and learning on your students' faces. See and *feel* yourself smiling as you're packing up your classroom at the end of the year, filled with a sense of pride for your self-discipline to follow through, knowing you had the best year possible. In other words, visualize yourself doing what you must do and thoroughly enjoying the process, especially if it's a process you don't naturally enjoy. Imagine what it would look and feel like if you *did* enjoy it.

Picture the look of determination on your face as you confidently and consistently connect with your students, listen to their needs, and take action based on what you observe. Visualize your students, their parents, your fellow teachers, and the administration responding to your positive demeanor and optimistic outlook. Even if you've had challenges in the past, visualize the outcome you actually want, and you might just be surprised when it really happens! Success first begins in your mind, with the mental movie you run in advance of an actual event.

Seeing yourself as the teacher who has it all together is the first step in actually getting it all together. Imagine yourself joyfully sitting down with your planner and organizing the upcoming days and weeks with lessons and classes. Visualize yourself driving home each day feeling happy and accomplished, knowing you had a day well done with students who will remember you for the rest of their lives because of the positive impact you had on them.

## Final Thoughts on Visualization

When you combine reading your affirmations every morning with daily visualization, you will turbocharge the programming of your subconscious mind for success through peak performance. When you visualize daily, you align your thoughts, feelings, and behaviors with your vision. This makes it easier to maintain the motivation you need to continue taking the necessary actions. Visualization can be a powerful aid in overcoming self-limiting beliefs—as well as self-limiting habits, such as procrastination—and get you into the actions necessary to achieve extraordinary results.

## E is for Exercise

Exercise should be a staple of your Miracle Morning. Even a few minutes of exercise each day significantly enhances your health, improves your self-confidence and emotional well-being, and enables you to think better and concentrate longer. You'll also notice how quickly your energy increases with daily exercise, and your students will notice your renewed energy (and theirs, too).

Personal development experts and self-made multimillionaire entrepreneurs Eben Pagan and Tony Robbins (who is also a bestselling author) both agree that the number one key to success is to start every morning with a personal success ritual. Included in both of their success rituals is some type of morning exercise. Eben articulates the importance of *morning* exercise: "Every morning, you've got to get your heart rate up and get your blood flowing and fill your lungs with oxygen." He continued, "Don't just exercise at the end of the day, or in the middle of the day. And even if you do like to exercise at those times, always incorporate at least 10 to 20 minutes of jumping jacks, or some sort of aerobic exercise, in the morning." Hey, if it works for Eben and Tony, it will work for me (and you)!

Lest you think you must engage in triathlon or marathon training, think again. Your morning exercise also doesn't need to replace an afternoon or evening regimen if you already have one in place. You can still hit the gym at the usual time. However, the benefits from adding as little as five minutes of morning exercise are undeniable, including improved blood pressure and blood sugar levels and decreased risk of all kinds of scary things like heart disease, osteoporosis, cancer, and diabetes. Maybe most importantly, a little exercise in the morning will increase your energy levels for the rest of the day to help you keep up with your demanding schedule.

You can go for a walk or run, follow along to a yoga video on YouTube, or find a Life S.A.V.E.R.S. buddy and play some early morning racquetball. There's also an excellent app called 7 Minute Workout that gives you a full-body workout in—you guessed it— seven minutes. The choice is yours, but pick one activity and do it.

As a teacher, you are constantly on the go. You need an endless reserve of energy to make the best of the challenges that come your way, and a daily morning exercise practice is going to provide it.

## Exercise for Your Brain

Even if you don't care about your physical health, consider that exercise is simply going to make you smarter, and that can only help your problem-solving abilities. Dr. Steven Masley, a Florida physician and nutritionist with a health practice geared toward executives, explains how exercise creates a direct connection to your cognitive ability.

"If we're talking about brain performance, the best predictor of brain speed is aerobic capacity—how well you can run up a hill is very strongly correlated with brain speed and cognitive shifting ability," Masley said.

Masley has designed a corporate wellness program based on the work he's done with more than 1,000 patients. "The average person going into these programs will increase brain speed by 25–30 percent."

Hal chose yoga for his exercise activity and began practicing it shortly after he created the Miracle Morning. He's been doing it and loving it ever since. Our exercise routines differ. I start each day with ten to twenty minutes of yoga, then do a second workout consisting of cardio, strength training, or both after the end of my workday.

# Final Thoughts on Exercise

You know that if you want to maintain good health and increase your energy, you must exercise consistently. That's not news to anyone. But what also isn't news is how easy it is to make excuses. Two of the biggest are "I don't have time" and "I'm too tired." And those are just the first two on the list. There is no limit to the excuses you can think of. And the more creative you are, the more excuses you can find!

That's the beauty of incorporating exercise into your Miracle Morning—it happens before your day wears you out and before you have an entire day to come up with new excuses. Because it comes first, the Miracle Morning is a surefire way to avoid those excuses and make exercise a daily habit.

Legal disclaimer: Hopefully this goes without saying, but you should consult your doctor or physician before beginning any exercise regimen, especially if you are experiencing any physical pain, discomfort, disabilities, etc. You may need to modify or even refrain from an exercise routine to meet your individual needs.

# R is for Reading

One of the fastest ways to achieve everything you want is to find successful people to be your role models. For every goal you have, there's a good chance an expert out there has already achieved the same thing or something similar. As Tony Robbins says, "Success leaves clues."

Fortunately, some of the best of the best have shared their stories in writing. And that means all those success blueprints are just waiting for anyone willing to invest the time in reading. Books are a limitless supply of help and mentorship right at your fingertips.

If you are already a reader, great! But if you haven't picked up a book since your last assigned reading in school, you have an incredible opportunity here.

Although reading doesn't *directly* produce results (at least not in the short term), there are many activities that can pull us in other, lower-level and less fruitful, directions. These benefit us far less in the long run than a consistent reading habit.

Want to go from zero to millionaire in no time flat? Want to learn how to think and grow rich? Ready to awaken the giant within? Be happy for no reason? Implement a four-hour work week? Double your revenue and profit in three years or less? You're in luck… I've heard that several authors have written books on precisely those topics.

Occasionally, I hear someone say, "I'm so busy, I don't have time to read." I get it. I used to have that belief as well. But now I think of what my mentor used to say: "The greatest minds in human history have spent years condensing the best of what they know into a few pages that can be purchased for a few dollars, read in a few hours, and shorten your learning curve by decades. But I get it ... you're too busy." Ouch!

It's worthwhile to find one, ten, or even twenty minutes every day to take in valuable content to enrich your life. Just use some of the strategies shared earlier in this book, spend five less minutes on Facebook before you start your day, or eat lunch while reading to nourish your mind and body simultaneously.

Here are some books Hal and I suggest you start with, and once you've primed your reading pump, we bet you'll keep going and never stop!

## On Teaching:

- *What Great Teachers Do Differently: 17 Things that Matter Most* by Todd Whitaker

- *Courage to Grow: How Acton Academy Turns Learning Upside Down* by Laura Sandefer

- *Take Control of the Noisy Class: Chaos to Calm in 15 Seconds* by Rob Plevin

- *Kids Deserve It: Pushing Boundaries and Challenging Conventional Thinking* by Todd Nesloney and Adam Welcome

- *Teach Like a Pirate: Increase Student Engagement, Boost Your Creativity, and Transform Your Life as an Educator* by Dave Burgess

- *Ditch that Textbook: Free Your Teaching and Revolutionize Your Classroom* by Matt Miller

- *Amplify: Digital Teaching and Learning in the K-6 Classroom* by Katie Muhtaris and Kristin Ziemke

- *The Innovator's Mindset: Empower Learning, Unleash Talent, and Lead a Culture of Creativity* by George Couros

- *The Book Whisperer: Awakening the Inner Reader in Every Child* by Donalyn Miller

- *Sparks in the Dark: Lessons, Ideas, and Strategies to Illuminate the Reading and Writing Lives in All of Us* by Todd Nesloney and Travis Crowder

- *Game Changer!: Book Access for All Kids* by Donalyn Miller and Colby Sharp

- *Mindsets in the Classroom: Building a Growth Mindset Learning Community* by Mary Cay Ricci

- *Lost at School: Why Our Kids with Behavioral Challenges are Falling Through the Cracks and How We Can Help Them* by Ross W. Greene

- *Teaching with Love & Logic: Taking Control of the Classroom* by Jim Fay and David Funk

## On Mindset:

- *The Art of Exceptional Living* by Jim Rohn

- *The One Thing: The Surprisingly Simple Truth Behind Extraordinary Results* by Gary Keller and Jay Papasan

- *The 7 Habits of Highly Effective People: Powerful Lessons in Personal Change* by Stephen R. Covey

- *Mastery* by Robert Greene

- *The Game of Life and How to Play It* by Florence Scovel Shinn

- *The Compound Effect: Jumpstart Your Income, Your Life, Your Success* by Darren Hardy

- *Think and Grow Rich* by Napoleon Hill

- *Finding Your Element: How to Discover Your Talents and Passions and Transform Your Life* by Sir Ken Robinson, PhD, and Lou Aronica

- *Spirit Led Instead: The Little Tool Book of Limitless Transformation* by Jenai Lane

- *Vision to Reality: How Short Term Massive Action Equals Long Term Maximum Results* and *Business Dating: Applying*

*Relationship Rules in Business for Ultimate Success* by Honorée Corder

- *Taking Life Head On: How to Love the Life You Have While You Create the Life of Your Dreams* by Hal Elrod

In addition to finding teaching confidence, you can transform your relationships, increase your self-confidence, improve your communication skills, learn how to become healthy, and improve any other area of your life you can think of. Head to your library or local bookstore, ask trusted colleagues and close friends—or do what we do and visit Amazon.com—and you'll find more books than you can possibly imagine on any area of your life you want to improve.

For a complete list of Hal's favorite personal development books—including those that have made the biggest impact on his success and happiness—check out the Recommended Reading list at TMMBook.com.

## How Much Should You Read?

I recommend making a commitment to read a minimum of ten pages per day (although five is okay to start with if you read slowly or don't yet enjoy reading).

Ten pages may not seem like a lot, but let's do the math. Reading ten pages per day adds up to 3,650 pages per year, which stacks up to approximately eighteen 200-page books that will enable you to take yourself to the next level so that you can take your success to the next level. All in just ten to fifteen minutes of daily reading, or fifteen to thirty minutes if you read more slowly.

Let me ask you, if you read eighteen personal and/or professional development books in the next twelve months, do you think you'll improve your mindset, gain more confidence, and learn proven strategies that will accelerate your success? Do you think you'll be a better, more capable version of who you are today? Do you think that will be reflected in your teaching results? Absolutely! Reading ten pages per day is not going to break you, but it will absolutely make you.

## Final Thoughts on Reading

- Begin with the end in mind—what do you hope to gain from the book? Take a moment to do this now by asking yourself what you want to gain from reading this one.

- Books don't have to be read cover to cover, nor do they have to be finished. Remember that this is *your* reading time. Use the table of contents to make sure you are reading the parts you care about most, and don't hesitate to put it down and move to another book if you aren't enjoying it. There is too much incredible information out there to spend any time on the mediocre.

- Many Miracle Morning practitioners use their reading time to catch up on their religious texts, such as the Bible or the Torah.

- Unless you're borrowing a book from the library or a friend, feel free to underline, circle, highlight, dog-ear, and take notes in the margins of the book. The process of marking books as you read allows you to come back at any time and recapture the key lessons, ideas, and benefits without needing to read the book again cover to cover. If you read on a digital reader, such as Kindle, Nook, or via iBooks, notes and highlighting are easily organized, so you can see them each time you flip through the book, or you can go directly to a list of your notes and highlights.

- Summarize key ideas, insights, and memorable passages in a journal. You can build your own summary of your favorite books so you can revisit the key content any time in just minutes.

- Rereading good personal development books is an underused yet very effective strategy. Rarely can you read a book once and internalize all its value. Achieving mastery in any area requires repetition. I've read *Spirit Led Instead* by Jenai Lane as many as three times and often refer to it throughout the year. Why not try it out with this book? Commit to rereading it as soon as you're finished to deepen your learning and give yourself more time to master your Miracle Morning.

- Audiobooks count as reading! You still get the information, and you can do it while exercising or during your commute. When I really want to study a book, I listen to the audio while looking at the text. This way I can take notes and underline text without slowing down too much. I am a pretty slow reader, but with audiobooks, I can listen at 1.5X or 2X speed and read much faster.

- Most importantly, quickly implement what you read. Schedule time to implement what you're reading, *while you're reading it.* Literally read with your schedule next to you, and schedule time blocks to put the content into action. Don't become a personal development junkie who reads a lot but does very little. I've met many people who take pride in the number of books they read, like some badge of honor. I'd rather read and implement one good book than to read ten books and then do nothing other than start reading the eleventh book. While reading is a great way to gain knowledge, insights, and strategies, it is the implementation and practice of these new strategies that will advance your life and career. Are you committed to implementing what you're learning in this book by taking action and following through with the 30-Day Challenge at the end?

Glad to hear it. Let's get to the final "S" of the S.A.V.E.R.S.

## S is for Scribing

Scribing is simply another word for writing. Let's keep it real—Hal needed an "S" for the end of S.A.V.E.R.S. because a "W" wouldn't fit anywhere. Thanks, Thesaurus®; we owe you one.

The scribing element of your Miracle Morning enables you to write down what you're grateful for and document your insights, ideas, breakthroughs, realizations, successes, and lessons learned, as well as any areas of opportunity, personal growth, or improvement.

Most Miracle Morning practitioners scribe in a journal for five to ten minutes during their Miracle Morning. By getting your thoughts out of your head and putting them in writing, you'll immediately gain heightened awareness, renewed clarity, and valuable insights to which you'd otherwise be oblivious.

If you're like Hal used to be, you probably have at least a few half-used and barely touched journals and notebooks. It wasn't until he started his own Miracle Morning practice that scribing quickly became one of his favorite daily habits. As Tony Robbins has said many times, "A life worth living is a life worth recording."

Writing will give you the daily benefits of consciously directing your thoughts, but what's even more powerful are the insights you'll gain from reviewing your journals, from cover to cover, afterwards—especially at the end of the year.

It is hard to put into words how overwhelmingly constructive the experience of going back and reviewing your journals can be. Michael Maher, *The Miracle Morning for Real Estate Agents* coauthor, is an avid practitioner of the Life S.A.V.E.R.S. Part of Michael's morning routine is to write down his appreciations and affirmations in what he calls his Blessings Book. Michael says it best:

"What you appreciate … APPRECIATES. It is time to take our insatiable appetite for what we want and replace it with an insatiable appetite and gratitude for what we do have. Write your appreciations, be grateful and appreciative, and you will have more of those things you crave—better relationships, more material goods, more happiness."

There is strength in writing down what you appreciate, and reviewing this material can change your mindset on a challenging day. A great practice to add to your routine is to write what you appreciate about each of your children, your significant other, and especially yourself. When we write down the things we appreciate about our loved ones, even (and particularly) when they are not on their best behavior, it's easier to focus on their positive qualities.

For example, you may be angry with your son because he hit your daughter, but let's say you notice that he attempted to comfort her afterwards. While you can discipline the hitting behavior, it's important to also notice his compassion after the fact. Another example would be when your spouse is late for your date night. It would be easy to get angry, but instead you can feel grateful that he arrived safely and that you're out of the house and get to enjoy alone time away from the kids!

While there are many worthwhile benefits of keeping a daily journal, here are a few more of my favorites. With daily scribing, you'll:

**Gain Clarity**—Journaling will give you more clarity and understanding of your past and current circumstances and help you work through challenges you're facing. At the same time, journaling allows you to brainstorm, prioritize, and plan your actions each day in order to optimize your future.

- **Capture Ideas**—You will be able to capture, organize, and expand on your ideas and keep from losing the important ones you are saving for an opportune moment in the future.

- **Review Lessons**—Journaling provides a place to record, reference, and review the lessons you've learned, both from your wins and any mistakes you make along the way.

- **Acknowledge Your Progress**—Going back and rereading your journal entries from a year—or even a week—ago, and seeing how much progress you've made, can be hugely beneficial. It truly is one of the most enjoyable, eye-opening, and confidence-inspiring experiences, and it can't be duplicated any other way.

- **Improve Your Memory**—People always think they will remember things, but if you've ever gone to the grocery store without a list, you know this is simply untrue. When we write something down, we are much more likely to remember it, and if we forget, we can always go back and read it again.

# Effective Journaling

Here are three simple steps to get started with journaling or improve your current journaling process.

**First...**Choose a format: physical or digital. You'll want to decide up front if you prefer a traditional, physical journal or a digital journal (on your computer or an app for your phone or tablet). If you aren't sure, experiment with both and see which feels best.

**Second...**Get a journal. Almost anything can work, but when it comes to a physical journal, there is something to be said for an attractive, durable one that you enjoy looking at; after all, ideally, you're going to have it for the rest of your life. I like to buy nice leather journals with lines on the pages, but it's your journal, so choose what works best for you. Some people prefer journals without lines so they can draw or create mind maps. Others like to have one page for each day of the year that is predated to help them stay accountable.

Here are a few favorite physical journals from TMM Facebook Community:

*The Five-Minute Journal* (FiveMinuteJournal.com) has become popular among top performers. It has a very specific format for each day with prompts, such as "I am grateful for …" and "What would make today great?" It takes five minutes or less and includes an evening option so you can review your day.

- *The Freedom Journal* (TheFreedomJournal.com) gives you a structured daily process that is focused on helping you with a single objective: *Accomplish Your #1 Goal in 100 Days.* Beautifully designed by John Lee Dumas of Entrepreneur On Fire, it's designed specifically to help you set and accomplish one big goal at a time.

- The Plan: *Your Legendary Life Planner* (LegendaryLifePlan.com) was designed by friends of ours. It is a goal-setting and habit-tracking system and planner for people who are ready for life balance and are willing to be intentional about achieving level ten in all areas of life.

- *The Miracle Morning Journal* (MiracleMorningJournal.com) is designed specifically to enhance and support your Miracle Morning, to keep you organized and accountable, and to track your S.A.V.E.R.S. each day. You can also download a free sample of *The Miracle Morning Journal* today at TMMBook. com to make sure it's right for you.

- If you prefer to use a digital journal, many choices are available. Here are a few favorites:

*The Five-Minute Journal* (FiveMinuteJournal.com) also offers an iPhone app, which follows the same format as the physical version but allows you to upload photographs to your daily entries. It also sends you helpful reminders to input your entries each morning and evening.

- *Day One* (DayOneApp.com) is a popular journaling app, and it's perfect if you don't want any structure or any limits on how much you can write. Day One offers a blank page for each daily entry, so if you like to write lengthy journal entries, this may be the app for you.

- *Penzu* (Penzu.com) is a popular online journal that doesn't require an iPhone, iPad, or Android device. All you need is a computer.

- Again, it really comes down to your preference and the features you want. If none of these digital options resonate with you, type "online journal" into Google, or simply type "journal" into the app store, and you'll get a variety of choices.

**Third...**Scribe daily. There are endless things you can write about—notes on the book you're reading, a list of things you're grateful for, and your top three to five priorities for the day are a good place to start. Write whatever makes you feel good and optimizes your day. Don't worry about grammar, spelling, or punctuation.

Your journal is a place to let your imagination run wild, so keep a muzzle on your inner critic. Don't edit—just scribe!

## Customizing Your S.A.V.E.R.S.

I know that you might have days when you can't do the Miracle Morning practice all at once. Feel free to split up the Life S.A.V.E.R.S. in any way that works for you. I want to share a few ideas specifically geared toward customizing the Life S.A.V.E.R.S. based on your schedule and preferences. Your current morning routine might allow you to fit in only a six-, twenty-, or thirty-minute Miracle Morning, or you might choose to do a longer version on the weekends.

Here is an example of a common sixty-minute Miracle Morning schedule using the Life S.A.V.E.R.S.:

**S**ilence: ten minutes

**A**ffirmations: five minutes

**V**isualization: five minutes

**E**xercise: ten minutes

**R**eading: twenty minutes

**S**cribing: ten minutes

You can customize the sequence, too. I prefer to do my reading and scribing first because it takes the most focus, which is hard to come by if I'm interrupted. Hal prefers to start with a period of peaceful, purposeful silence so that he can wake up slowly, clear his mind, and focus his energy and intentions. However, this is your Miracle Morning, not ours; feel free to experiment with different sequences to see which you like best.

## Ego Depletion and Your Miracle Morning

Have you ever wondered why you can resist sugary snacks in the morning, but your resistance crumbles in the afternoon or evening? Why is it that sometimes our willpower is strong and other times it deserts us? It turns out that willpower is like a muscle that grows tired from use, and at the end of the day, it is harder to push ourselves to do activities that serve us and avoid those that don't. It also means we have less patience for our loved ones in the afternoon and evening, when they could probably use it the most.

The good news is that we know how this works and can set ourselves up for success with some advanced planning. And the great news? The Miracle Morning is an integral part of your plan. To see how this works, we need to understand ego depletion.

Ego depletion is a term to describe "a person's diminished capacity to regulate their thoughts, feelings, and actions," according to Roy F. Baumeister and John Tierney, the authors of *Willpower*. Ego depletion grows worse at the end of the day and when we are hungry, tired, or have had to exert our willpower too often.

If you wait until the end of the day to do important things that give you energy and help you become the person you want to be, you'll find that your excuses are more compelling and your motivation has gone missing. But, when you wake up and do your Miracle Morning first thing, you gain the increased energy and mindfulness that the Life S.A.V.E.R.S. routine provides and keep ego depletion from getting in your way.

When you perform the Life S.A.V.E.R.S. habit every day, you learn the mechanics of habit formation when your willpower is strongest, and you can use this knowledge and energy to adopt small and doable habits at other times of the day.

## Final Thoughts on the Life S.A.V.E.R.S.

Everything is difficult before it's easy. Every new experience is uncomfortable before it's comfortable. The more you practice the Life S.A.V.E.R.S., the more natural and normal each of them will feel. Hal's first time meditating was almost his last, because his mind raced like a Ferrari and his thoughts bounced around uncontrollably like the silver sphere in a pinball machine. Now, he loves meditation, and while he's still no master, he says he's decent at it.

Similarly, I had trouble with affirmations when I first started my Miracle Mornings. I didn't know what I wanted to affirm. So, I stole a few from *The Miracle Morning* and added a few that came to mind. It was okay, but they didn't really *mean* much to me initially. Over time, as I encountered things that struck me as powerful, I added them to my affirmations and adjusted the ones I had. Now, my affirmations mean a lot to me, and the daily act of using them is far more powerful.

In fact, I used the affirmation, "I am fully committed to writing *The Miracle Morning for Teachers* this year by sticking to my deadlines and protecting time to write" to motivate myself daily to finish this very book!

I invite you to begin practicing the Life S.A.V.E.R.S. now, so you can become familiar and comfortable with each of them and get a jump-start before you begin The Miracle Morning 30-Day Challenge.

# The Six-Minute Miracle Morning

If your biggest concern is still finding time, don't worry; I've got you covered. You can do the entire Miracle Morning—receiving the full benefits of all six S.A.V.E.R.S.—in only six minutes a day, literally. While six minutes isn't the duration I'd recommend on a daily basis, on those days when you're pressed for time, simply do each of the S.A.V.E.R.S. for one minute each. In fact, when we invited your teaching colleagues to bring the S.A.V.E.R.S. into their classrooms, we asked *only* for a six-minute daily commitment (knowing you couldn't add an entire hour to your regular daily instruction). The stories you'll read in this book show, beyond a shadow of a doubt, that a six-minute daily S.A.V.E.R.S. practice can make a world of difference!

Here is a suggested sequence for you, and we've provided instructions for how to share the S.A.V.E.R.S. with your students in *The Miracle Morning for Teachers' User Guide*, which you can download here.

**Minute One (S):** Close your eyes and enjoy a moment of peaceful, purposeful silence to clear your mind and get centered for your day.

**Minute Two (A):** Read your most important affirmation to reinforce *what* result you want to accomplish, *why* it's important to you, *which* specific actions you must take, and, most importantly, precisely *when* you will commit to taking those actions

**Minute Three (V):** Visualize yourself flawlessly executing the single most important action that you want to mentally rehearse for the day.

**Minute Four (E):** Stand up and engage in some high-energy jumping jacks, or drop and do push-ups and/or crunches, to get your heart rate up and engage your physiology.

**Minute Five (R):** Grab the book you're reading and read a page, or a paragraph, and finally…

**Minute Six (S):** Grab your journal, and jot down one thing for which you're grateful, along with the single most important result for you to generate that day.

I'm sure you can see how, even in just six minutes, the S.A.V.E.R.S. will set you on the right path for the day—and you can always devote more time later when your schedule permits or the opportunity presents itself. Doing the six-minute practice is a way to start a mini habit to build up your confidence or to bookmark the habit on a tough morning. Another mini habit you could do is to start with just *one* of the Life S.A.V.E.R.S. (in fact, right now you're in the midst of implementing the "R" for Reading), and once you get used to waking up earlier, add more of them. Remember that the goal is to have some time to work on your personal goals and mindset, so if you are overwhelmed, it's not going to work for you.

Personally, my Miracle Morning has grown into a daily ritual of renewal and inspiration that I absolutely love! In the coming chapters, I will cover *a lot* of information that has the potential to take both your impact as a teacher and your quality of life to new levels, and I can't wait to share this with you.

## Meet Legendary Teacher-Contributor
# Candace Kluba
### Campbellton Elementary, Third Grade

Upon completion of our first month of using the Life S.A.V.E.R.S., my students remained excited about their silent time and kept asking for more extended periods of silence. I don't know about you, but I cannot remember the last time I heard an eight-year-old ask for silent time! They love their minute of silence. I honestly have no idea what they might be thinking of during this time. The truth is that I don't even care! If I agree to their request, I can easily get up to an additional minute or more of silence from my entire class. There is no other time of day when my students get to enjoy a minute of peace and quiet that is also free from any expectations. They appreciate their one opportunity to sit in complete silence with just their minds.

My students have also grown especially fond of the minutes they use for reading and scribing. They get upset if they are not able to complete a reading assignment within one minute. They also keep track of how much writing they do each day and always look for more time to write. Before we began the Life S.A.V.E.R.S. program, my students were already using daily affirmations. However, these felt automated, as my students were reciting them without any emotion. When we started the Life S.A.V.E.R.S. in their entirety, I had my students create their unique affirmations. The result is that they are much more invested in these than they ever were with the ones I had written for them at the beginning of the school year.

My students have even requested a minute of exercise followed by a minute of silence after returning from lunch as a sort of mini Life S.A.V.E.R.S. program. They appreciate taking a moment to calm their bodies and return their focus to the classroom environment before resuming their learning. My students have not dramatically changed, as it has only been a month. However, they continue to build good habits by enjoying the S.A.V.E.R.S. program each day. They continue to practice sitting in silence and breathing to align their minds and hearts. They are discovering that these daily routines benefit them by teaching the habits of successful people at a young age. If they continue to utilize these strategies, their success will be guaranteed.

## Meet Legendary Teacher-Contributor
# Charlotte Council
### Homeschool Teacher & Mom to Six

My experiment for *The Miracle Morning for Teachers* book is probably a bit different than most. I have had the privilege of graduating five of our six homeschooled children. I'm currently homeschooling my youngest teenage son, Ethan.

After trying *The Miracle Morning* Life S.A.V.E.R.S. last year without an accountability partner, I found myself unable to stick with the plan. I was extremely excited for the chance to introduce this concept to my son. Having a partner was just what I needed to create positive change in my life. Ethan was willing to spend a few minutes of his day working with me on our new project.

From the beginning, we realized that finding time to get together consistently in the mornings would be difficult. Because of our schedules, our Miracle Morning occurred mostly in the evenings. Some days we were on our own, but we still held each other accountable.

As an expression of our faith in Jesus Christ, we prayed during our time of silence. We also discussed the many benefits for those who practice meditation.

Affirmations were a new concept for Ethan. Every day, we would write as many affirmations in our journals as time would allow. Writing and believing positive statements about ourselves became an essential exercise for both of us.

Goal setting is something I have struggled with for some time. We both now understand that having goals gives direction and purpose. Ethan saw the benefits right away. He has now picked up on the idea that with a plan in place, he could cultivate his dreams into reality. He will continue to pursue the goals he has for himself as well as create new ones.

A good stretching routine turned out to be a physical activity that we could do together. We found that stretching, even for just a minute, seemed to be just enough to give us a boost of energy.

I love reading for my personal development, so it wasn't hard to choose a book for me to read. Because Ethan isn't an avid reader, I chose *Think and Grow Rich* by Napoleon Hill for him. It was a book that would stimulate his thoughts about himself and his future. Reading helps develop our thoughts and gives us endless knowledge and lessons while keeping our minds active.

The daily habit of writing down our affirmations allowed Ethan and me to become more in tune with who we are and what we want to achieve. The practice of daily journaling provides a great visual aid to see what one has accomplished. It is part of the blueprint for realizing dreams.

Toward the end of our experiment for *The Miracle Morning for Teachers*, Ethan said that writing the affirmations down had the most significant impact on him. Developing statements that reflect his personality, goals, and dreams became a game for him. He feels he is now on the right track to achieving success. He wants to share his Miracle Morning experience with others, especially his peers.

# SECTION 2:

# THE NOT-SO-OBVIOUS
# LEGENDARY TEACHER PRINCIPLES

# — 4 —

# NOT-SO-OBVIOUS LEGENDARY TEACHER PRINCIPLE #1:

## SELF-LEADERSHIP

*Your level of success will seldom exceed
your level of personal development,
because success is something you attract
by the person you become.*

—JIM ROHN

We've been lied to. Yep. Society has conditioned all of us to think that the way to *have* more is to *do* more.

Want more money? Work harder. Put in *more* hours.

Want more happiness? Do more of the things that bring you joy.

Want more love? Do *more* for your partner than they do for you.

But what if the real secret to having more of what we want in our lives is not about *doing* more but *becoming* more?

It is this philosophy that gave birth to, and remains the foundation of, the Miracle Morning: *our levels of success in every single area of our lives is determined by our levels of personal development* (i.e. our beliefs, knowledge, emotional intelligence, skills, abilities, faith, etc.) in each area. So, if we want to have more, we must first become more.

Think of it this way: if you were to measure your desired level of success, on a scale of one to ten, in every area of your life, it's safe to say that you want "level ten" success in each area. I've never met anyone who honestly said, "Nah, I don't want to be too happy...too healthy...or too wealthy...I am content just settling for less than my potential and cruising along with a level five life."

The question is: what are you doing each day to first become a level ten person?

In other words, who you're becoming is far more important than what you're doing, and yet the irony is that what you're doing, each day, is determining who you're becoming.

Andrew Bryant, founder of Self-Leadership International, summed it up this way: "Self-leadership is the practice of intentionally influencing your thinking, feeling, and behaviors to achieve your objective(s) ... [It] is having a developed sense of who you are, what you can do, and where you are going, coupled with the ability to influence your communication, emotions, and behaviors on the way to getting there."

Before I reveal the key principles of self-leadership, I want to share with you what I've discovered about the crucial role that your *mindset* plays as the foundation of effective self-leadership. Your past beliefs, self-image, and ability to collaborate with and rely upon others at integral times will factor into your ability to excel as a self-leader.

## Be Aware—and Skeptical—of Your Self-Imposed Limitations

You may be holding on to false limiting beliefs that are unconsciously interfering with your ability to achieve your personal and professional goals.

For example, you may be someone who repeats, "I wish I were more organized," or, "I'm not an organized person." Yet you are more than capable of providing the structure and inspiration to be organized. Thinking of yourself as less than capable assumes imminent failure and simultaneously thwarts your ability to succeed. Life contains enough obstacles without your creating more for yourself!

Effective self-leaders closely examine their beliefs, decide which ones serve them, and eliminate the ones that don't.

When you find yourself stating anything that sounds like a limiting belief, from "I don't have enough time" to "I could never do that," pause and turn your self-limiting statements into empowering questions. You might instead ask, *Where can I find more time in my schedule? How might I be able to do that?*

Revising limiting beliefs allows you to tap into your inborn creativity and find solutions. You can always find a way when you're committed. As tennis star Martina Navratilova said, "The difference between involvement and commitment is like ham and eggs. The chicken is involved; the pig is committed." Being all in is the key to making anything happen.

## See Yourself as Better than You've Ever Been

As Hal wrote in *The Miracle Morning*, most of us suffer from Rearview Mirror Syndrome, limiting our current and future results based on who we were in the past. Remember that, although *where you are is a result of who you were, where you go depends entirely on the person you choose to be from this moment forward.* This is especially important for teachers. You will make mistakes. Don't let your sense of guilt about that keep you from looking forward. Learn from your mistakes and do better next time.

I watched an interview with Sara Blakely, the founder of Spanx and the youngest self-made female billionaire in the United States. She attributes her success to a mindset her father instilled in her. "When I was growing up, he encouraged us to fail," she said. "We'd come home from school and at dinner he'd say: 'What did you fail at today?' And if there was nothing, he'd be disappointed. It was an interesting kind of reverse psychology. I would come home and say that I tried out for something and I was just horrible and he high fived me." If we allow them to be, our mistakes can turn into our greatest lessons.

We all make mistakes! As human beings, we do not come with instruction manuals, and there will always be someone with an unsolicited opinion about the way you are living your life. Don't listen to the static! Be confident in your choices, and when you aren't sure, find the answers and support you need.

All successful people made the choice to see themselves as better than they had ever been before. They stopped maintaining limiting beliefs based on their past and instead started forming beliefs based on their unlimited potential.

One of the best ways to do this is to follow the four-step Miracle Morning Affirmations formula for creating results-oriented affirmations as outlined in the last chapter. Be sure to create affirmations that reinforce what's possible for you. Remind yourself of your ideal outcome, why it's important to you, which actions you're committed to taking to achieve it, and precisely when you're committed to taking those actions.

## Actively Seek Support

Seeking support is crucial for teachers. Even so, many struggle, suffering in silence because they assume everyone else has greater capabilities, and they all but refuse to seek help and assistance.

People who are self-leaders know they can't do it alone. You might need moral support, for example, so you can replenish the energy stores that life is so famous for depleting. Or you may need accountability support to overcome your tendency to disengage when the going gets tough. We all need support in different areas of our lives, and great self-leaders understand that and use it to their benefit.

The Miracle Morning Community on Facebook is a great place to start looking for support. The members are positive and responsive. Try joining a local group for people with similar goals and interests. Meetup.com is a great place to find like-minded folks who are close by. I highly recommend getting an accountability partner and, if you can, a life or business coach who can help you.

## The Five Foundational Principles of Self-Leadership

While self-leadership is a skill, all skills are built on a foundation of principles. To grow and reach the levels of success you aspire to reach, you'll need to become a proficient self-leader. My favorite way to cut the learning curve in half and decrease the time it takes you to reach the top 1 percent is to model the traits and behaviors of those who have reached the top before you.

I've seen many leaders and a myriad of effective strategies, as I'm sure you have. Here are the five principles I believe will make the biggest impact on your commitment to self-leadership:

**1.** Take 100 Percent Responsibility

**2.** Prioritize Fitness and Make Exercise Enjoyable

**3.** Aim for Financial Freedom

**4.** Systematize Your World

**5.** Commit to Your Result-Producing Process

## Principle #1: Take 100 Percent Responsibility

Here's the hard truth: if your life and career are not where you want them to be, it's all on you. .

The sooner you take ownership of that fact, the sooner you'll begin to move forward. This isn't meant to be harsh. Successful people are rarely victims. In fact, one of the reasons they are successful is that they take absolute, total, and complete responsibility for each and every single aspect of their lives—whether it's personal or professional, good or bad, their job or someone else's.

While victims habitually waste their time and energy blaming others and complaining, achievers are busy creating the results and circumstances they want for their lives. Mediocre teachers complain that none of their students are thriving for *this* reason or *that* reason, or that it's the administration's fault for underperforming students. In contrast, successful teachers take 100 percent responsibility for finding what works for their students and, more importantly, acquiring the skills necessary to build up their students and get them to not only pass the class but effectively learn the material. Teachers who accept responsibility are so busy focused on getting positive results they don't have time to complain.

I've heard Hal articulate a profound distinction during one of his keynote speeches: "The moment you take 100 percent responsibility for everything in your life is the same moment you claim your power to change anything in your life. However, the crucial distinction is to realize that taking responsibility is not the same thing as accepting *blame*. While blame determines who is at fault for something, responsibility determines who is committed to improving a situation. It rarely matters who is at fault. All that matters is that *you* are committed to improving your situation." He's right. And it's so empowering when you truly start to think and act accordingly. Suddenly, your life, and your results, are within your control.

When you take true ownership of your life, there's no time for discussing whose fault something is or who gets the blame. Playing the blame game is easy, but there's no longer any place for it in your life. Avoiding responsibility for why you didn't meet your goals, or why your students are failing, is for other teachers, not you. You own your results—good and bad. You can celebrate the good and learn from the so-called bad. Either way, you always have a choice about how you respond or react in any and every situation.

One of the reasons this mindset is so important is that you are leading by example. If you're always looking for someone else to the blame, your administration, colleagues, students, and their parents will see that, and they likely won't respect it (or you). Like a parent trying to bring out the best in their kids, the people you lead are always watching you, and it's crucial to live by the values that you want to instill in each of them.

Here's the psychological shift I suggest you make: take ownership and stewardship over all of your decisions, actions, and outcomes—starting right now. Replace unnecessary blame with unwavering responsibility. Even if someone else drops the ball, ask yourself what you could have done and, more importantly, what you can do in the future to prevent that ball from being dropped again. While you can't change what's in the past, the good news is that you can change everything else.

From now on, there's no doubt about who is at the wheel and who is responsible for all of your results. You make the calls, do the follow-up, decide the outcomes you want, and get the desired effects. Your results are 100 percent your responsibility. Right?

Remember: you are in the position of power, you are in control, and there are no limits to what you can accomplish.

## Principle #2: Prioritize Fitness and Make Exercise Enjoyable

On a scale of one to ten, where would you rank your health and fitness? Are you fit? Strong? Do you *feel* good, more often than not?

How about your energy level throughout the day? Do you have more energy than you know what to do with? Can you wake up before your alarm and do what's important, handle all the demands of the day, and put out the inevitable fires, all without struggling to make it through the day or feeling exhausted and out of breath?

We covered exercise as the "E" in S.A.V.E.R.S., and yes, I'm going to discuss it again right now. It's a fact that the state of your health and fitness is a huge factor in your energy and success levels—especially for teachers. Let's face it, you're not paid just based on the times you clock in and out, or the time you're actually teaching. You're paid based on the quality of the results you produce within the time that you work. Being a terrific teacher is truly an energy sport. As with any sport, you need an extraordinary supply of energy and stamina.

It's no surprise, then, that three priorities of top performers—each of which you must prioritize in your life—are the quality of what they eat, how much they sleep, and how well they exercise. We'll delve deeper into each in the next chapter on *Energy Engineering*, but let's start with making sure you get your daily exercise in. The key is to find physical activities that you truly enjoy doing.

**Make exercise enjoyable.** The correlation between physical fitness, happiness, and success are undeniable. It is no coincidence that you rarely see top performers who are terribly out of shape. Most schedule and invest thirty to sixty minutes of their time each day to hit the gym or the running trail, because they understand the important role that daily exercise plays in their success.

While the "E" in S.A.V.E.R.S. ensures that you're going to start each day with five to ten minutes of exercise, we recommended that you make a commitment to engage in additional thirty- to sixty-minute workouts at least three to five times per week. Doing so will ensure that your fitness level supports the energy and confidence you need to succeed.

Even better is to engage in some form of exercise that brings you a deep level of enjoyment, whether that means going for a hike in nature, playing ultimate Frisbee, or getting an exercise bike and putting it in front of your TV so you can enjoy your favorite episode of *Breaking Bad* and forget that you're even exercising. Or, do what Hal does; he loves wakeboarding and playing basketball—two excellent forms of exercise—so he does one of them, every single workday. You'll see Hal's foundational schedule in the coming pages so you can get an idea of how those activities fit with the rest of his priorities.

Which physical activities do you enjoy that you can commit to scheduling as part of your daily exercise ritual?

## Principle #3: Aim for Financial Freedom

How does your journey toward financial freedom look? Do you earn significantly more money each month than you need to survive? Are you able to consistently save, invest, and contribute a significant portion of your income? Are you debt free with a large reserve that allows you to capitalize on opportunities that come your way and weather any unexpected financial storms? Are you on pace for financial freedom so that your ongoing passive income will exceed your ongoing monthly expenses? If so, congratulations. You are among a very small percentage of teachers who are genuinely thriving with their finances.

If not, you're not alone. Most people have less than $10,000 to their name and an average of $16,000 in unsecured debt. No judgment here if your finances are not yet where you want them to be. I'm simply going to point you right back to Principle #1 and encourage you to take 100 percent responsibility for your financial situation.

I've seen and heard every reason for someone to dive deep into debt, fail to save, and not have a nest egg. None of those matter now. Yes, the best time to have started saving a percentage of your income was five, ten, or even twenty years ago. But the next best time is right now. Whether you're twenty, forty, or sixty years old, it's never too late to take control of your personal finances. You'll find an incredible boost in energy from taking charge, and you'll be able to use your accumulated savings to create even more wealth because you'll have money to invest in new opportunities. Sounds good, right?

While it is highly unlikely your decision to become a teacher was driven by a desire for financial freedom, it is possible to obtain financial freedom even on a teacher's salary. It turns out that learning how to make money is only half the battle. Learning how to *keep* it by saving and investing wisely is the second part of the puzzle. Learning how to create multiple streams of income—so that you're never again dependent on one revenue source—is the next level, which we'll cover in the coming pages. Don't worry; if this is a new concept but one you find intriguing, there are several resources included in this book.

Financial freedom isn't something you achieve overnight. It is a result of developing the mindset and the habits *now* that will take you down the path that leads to financial freedom. Here are 4.8 practical steps you can start taking today to ensure that you are aiming your financial habits toward a future of financial freedom:

1. **Set aside 10 percent of your income to save and invest.**

    This is a must. In fact, I recommend that you start by taking 10 percent of whatever funds you have in the bank right now and putting it into a separate savings account. (Go ahead, I'll wait.) Make whatever adjustments you need to make to your lifestyle to be able to live off of 90 percent of your current income. A little discipline and sacrifice go a long way. Watching that 10 percent adding up over time will get exciting, and you'll start to *feel* what's possible for the future.

2. **Take another 10 percent and give it away.** Most wealthy people give a percentage of their income to causes they believe in. But you don't have to wait until you're wealthy to start this practice. Tony Robbins said, "If you won't give $1 out of $10, you'll never give $1 million out of $10 million." Can't do 10 percent or the rent check will bounce? Fine, start with 5, 2, or 1 percent. It's not the amount that matters, but developing the mindset and creating the habit will change your financial future and serve you for the rest of your life. You've got to start teaching your subconscious brain that it can produce an abundant income, that there's more than enough, and that there is always more on the way.

3. **Continuously develop your money mindset.** It's one of the most important topics for you to master, and you can start by adding the following books, which cover various aspects of financial freedom, to your reading list:

- *Wealth Can't Wait: Avoid the 7 Wealth Traps, Implement the 7 Business Pillars, and Complete a Life Audit Today by Miracle Morning Millionaires* co-author David Osborn and his co-author Paul Morris (both aforementioned books will be helpful for you)

- *Profit First: Transform Your Business from a Cash-Eating Monster to a Money-Making Machine* by Mike Michalowicz

- *Secrets of the Millionaire Mind: Mastering the Inner Game of Wealth* by T. Harv Eker

- *The Total Money Makeover: A Proven Plan for Financial Fitness* by Dave Ramsey

- *The Millionaire Fastlane: Crack the Code to Wealth and Live Rich for a Lifetime* by MJ DeMarco

- *MONEY: Master the Game: 7 Simple Steps to Financial Freedom* by Tony Robbins

- *Think and Grow Rich* by Napoleon Hill

- *Rich Dad Poor Dad* by Robert Kiyosaki

- *Magic Money Books 1-3: A Course in Creating Abundance* by Holly Alexander

4. **Diversify Your Sources of Income.** Whether you are a full-time teacher or you teach and have a side hustle, we assume know you value financial security in the present—and ultimately desire financial freedom in the as-soon-as-possible future. That means creating one or more additional streams of income is no longer a luxury. In today's unpredictable economy, it has become a necessity.

Diversifying your sources of income, also known as *creating multiple streams of income*, is one of the best decisions you can make. It is not only crucial to protect yourself and your family against the unavoidable ups and downs of economic and industry cycles but to establish a lifetime of financial independence. Due to the financial risks that come from relying on *one* source of income, we highly recommend creating one or more additional sources to generate cash flow.

At age twenty-five, Hal began planning his exit strategy to leave a lucrative Hall of Fame sales career to pursue his dream of becoming a full-time entrepreneur. While retaining his sales position and the income it generated, he started his first business. For his first additional stream of income, he provided sales coaching for both individual sales reps, and sales teams. When the economy crashed in 2008, Hal's income was almost entirely dependent on his coaching business. When more than half of his clients couldn't afford to pay for his coaching, and he lost over half of his income, he swore he'd never be dependent on one source of income again.

Year by year, using the exact step-by-step formula outlined below, Hal has since added nine additional, significant streams of income. These still include private coaching, as well as running group coaching programs, writing books, keynote speaking, facilitating paid masterminds, podcasting, foreign publishing, franchising and publishing books in *The Miracle Morning* book series, receiving affiliate income, and hosting live 300+-person events.

Your additional income streams can be active, passive, or a combination of the two. Some may pay you for doing work that you love (active), while others can provide income for you without your having to do much of anything at all (passive). You can diversify your income streams among different industries to protect you against major losses during downturns in one market and allow you to financially benefit from the upswings in another.

And while Hal's approach to creating multiple streams of income—mentioned above and outlined below—is just one of countless that you could take (e.g., you could buy real estate, leverage the stock market, do tutoring on the side, write books about your subject area expertise, etc.), the following steps (4.1-4.8) give you a practical, straightforward process that you can begin brainstorming and implementing immediately.

What's important is that you prioritize diversifying your sources of income. Schedule time blocks—one hour a day, one day a week, or a few hours every Saturday—so that you can begin to establish additional income sources that bring you additional monthly income. These sources will provide financial security in the present and ultimately financial freedom in the as-soon-as-possible future.

Here are the eight steps that Hal has repeatedly implemented, which you can apply or modify to fit your situation:

**4.1.** Establish financial security. Now, this step isn't sexy, but it's imperative. You might think of it as a disclaimer. Don't focus your time and energy into building a second source of income unless your primary source is secure. Focus on ensuring your primary monthly income will support your expenses before you pursue other steps. In other words, don't "burn the ships" like Cortés did, until you've at least established a rowboat that will keep you afloat while you're building your yacht.

**4.2. Clarify your unique value.** Every person on this planet has unique gifts, abilities, experiences, and value to offer in a way that adds value for others, and for which they can be highly compensated. Figure out the knowledge, experience, ability, or solution you have, or can create, which others will find value in and gladly pay you for. Remember, what might be common knowledge to you isn't for other people. Here are a few ways that you can differentiate your value in the marketplace.

**First...***who you are* and your unique personality will always differentiate your value from that of every other person on earth. Many people will resonate with your personality better than they will with someone else offering value that's similar or even the same.

**Second...***knowledge* is the one thing you can increase relatively quickly. As Tony Robbins wrote in *Money: Master the Game,* "One reason people succeed is that they have knowledge other people don't have. You pay your lawyer or your doctor for the knowledge and skills you lack."

Increasing your knowledge in a specific area is an effective way to increase the value that others will pay you for—either to teach them what you know, or to apply your knowledge on their behalf.

**Third...***packaging* is how you can differentiate your value. When Hal wrote *The Miracle Morning,* he admittedly had to overcome his insecurity around the fact that waking up early wasn't exactly something he invented. He wondered, would there really be a market for the book? But as hundreds of thousands of readers have shared, what made the book so impactful is the way that the information was packaged. It was simple and gave people a step-by-step process that made it possible for anyone to significantly improve any area of their life by simply altering how they start their day. How can you package your knowledge so it can benefit others and be turned into an additional stream of income?

4.3. **Identify your target audience.** Determine whom you are best qualified to serve. With his background as a record-breaking, Hall of Fame sales rep, Hal determined that he was best qualified to serve fellow sales reps, so he launched his first coaching program. Now he serves a much larger, worldwide audience through *The Miracle Morning* book series and *Best Year Ever Blueprint* live events. Meanwhile, I coach both first-time and established authors who want to create seven-figure incomes through their books and multiple other streams of income.

Consider the value you can add for others or the problems you can help people solve. Who will pay you for the value you can add for them, the solution you can provide, or the results you can help them generate?

4.4. **Build a self-sustaining community.** A turning point in Hal's financial life came when he heard self-made multimillionaire Dan Kennedy explain why one of the most valuable assets you'll ever have, as an entrepreneur, is your email list. So always focus on growing and nurturing it. At that time, Hal's email list was non-existent beyond his family and friends. However, he made it a priority.

Ten years later, in addition to taking Dan's advice and growing his email list to well over 100,000 loyal subscribers, he took it a step further by launching and growing one of the most engaged online communities in the world. The Miracle Morning Community on Facebook has become a case study, currently with over 200,000 members from 70+ countries and growing every day. It's not realistic for Hal to be able to facilitate engagement with that many people on his own, nor does he rely on his team to do it. Instead, through trial and error, he figured out how to automate both the growth of the community—to the tune of attracting more than 3,000 new members every month—and the member interaction. Now the community is able to sustain itself without his constant attention.

Here are a few tips from Hal on creating a self-sustaining community:

**First...**_choose your platform._ While it's important to focus on building your email list and communicating with your community individually, it's crucial that you establish a platform through which you can not only consistently add value but where members of your community can communicate with, and add value for, each other. While this can be facilitated through a membership platform such as Kajabi (Kajabi.com) or CMNTY (cmnty.com), Hal has found that using a Facebook group is advantageous for a few key reasons:

- Most people are already logging into Facebook every day.
- The built-in functionality of Facebook Groups allows self-managing.
- Other people who are on Facebook can stumble across your community.
- Your members can easily share your content, as well as each other's.

**Second...**_invite people to your community._ You may have noticed _A Special Invitation from Hal_ in the opening pages of this book. This section has been a staple in each of the *Miracle Morning* books and is the primary method that Hal uses to invite people to join the Facebook Group. Yours might be a "P.S." in your emails, or a clickable button on your website. In fact, if you go to MiracleMorning.com you'll also see a button there that says JOIN THE COMMUNITY and links back to the Facebook group. Whatever method you choose, make sure it's visible to your clients, prospects, and anyone else you'd like to have in your community.

**Third...***prompt your community to engage.* Start by giving all new members simple instructions that compel them to interact with—and add value for—other members. In the *Best Month Ever Challenge* (BMEC) Facebook group, there are four simple instructions:

1. Create a new post that shares your one area/goal/objective that you're committed to improving this month.

2. Leave a positive/encouraging/helpful comment on someone else's post.

3. Watch the BMEC videos [with links to the videos].

4. Post in the group daily [with specific instructions on what to post].

However, Hal recommends keeping it as simple as possible, such as using a POST and COMMENT model. Simply ask new members to *post* one thing that is relevant to them and the community, and then *comment* on someone else's post. This format creates a consistent flow of new posts and engagement within each member's post.

Another highly engaged online community is Jayson Gaignard's Mastermind Talks Alumni Facebook group, which is exclusively for attendees of his Mastermind Talks event (which happens to be where Hal and I met in person for the first time). Jayson guides member engagement with a simple ASK and GIVE model. You're either asking for something (advice, feedback, an introduction, etc.) or giving something (expertise, resources, conference tickets, etc.). This format has created a highly engaged, self-sustaining community where members provide ongoing support for one another.

**Fourth…***consistently add value.* Just because your community and its engagement are self-sustaining doesn't mean you should disengage. In fact, the more you engage, the better. This could be as simple as sharing valuable resources, or your own content, with your community. Hal posts his weekly podcast episode in the group every Wednesday and shares any valuable resources he comes across. You can also delegate your engagement as appropriate. Since Hal can't possibly "like" and "comment" on every person's post, he has his team engage as well. He has also appointed "Community Ambassadors" in various countries to engage with members in each of those countries.

4.5. **Ask your community about their challenges and desires.** Some people assume what people want and need, invest valuable time in creating what they *think* others need, and then *hope* that their guesses were correct. But remember: hope is rarely the best strategy.

A better approach is to send an email to members of your community, or put up a post in your group, with a survey link (using a free service like SurveyMonkey or Google Forms), asking what they want or need help within your area of expertise. Ask open-ended questions to help you later brainstorm, or offer multiple choices if you've already come up with ideas for what you can provide.

If you want to dive deeper into this topic, the most comprehensive resource on how to use surveys to assess what your prospects and customers want would be Ryan Levesque's book, *Ask: The Counterintuitive Online Formula to Discover Exactly What Your Customers Want to Buy… Create a Mass of Raving Fans… and Take Any Business to the Next Level.*

4.6. **Create a solution.** After your community members tell you what they need, here's your golden opportunity to get to work and create it. This could be a physical or digital product (a book, an audio recording, a video, a written training program or software) or a service (dog grooming, babysitting, coaching, consulting, speaking, or training).

**4.7. Plan the launch.** Think about how Apple rolls out its products. The company doesn't just throw a product on the shelf or its website. No, the company makes it into an event. Apple builds anticipation months in advance, so much so that people are willing to camp out in front of stores for weeks to be the first in line. Do that. To learn how, read the definitive book on the topic, *Launch* by Jeff Walker.

**4.8. Find a mentor.** Depending on your experience level, you may want to make this your *first* step. One of the most effective methods of minimizing your learning curve and maximizing the speed at which you attain a desired result is to find someone who has already achieved that result, determine how they did it, model their behavior, and modify it to fit your needs.

While you may seek a face-to-face or virtual relationship with a mentor, you could also join a mastermind and/or hire a coach. Even reading a book, like this one, is tapping into the wisdom of a mentor.

**Final thoughts…** Whether you follow these steps and create a new business or start buying investment properties, you'll want to schedule time to begin adding and developing another source of income. Within months, you can be enjoying the benefits, perks, financial security, peace of mind, and freedom that comes from having multiple streams of income. Two years from now, you'll wish you would have started today. Don't wish, and don't wait. Start now.

# Principle #4: Systematize Your World

Effective self-leaders have *systems* for just about everything, from work activities—such as scheduling, following up, preparing lesson plans, and sending thank-you cards—to personal activities, such as sleeping, eating, managing money, maintaining cars, and handling family responsibilities. Those systems make life easier and ensure you are ready for anything.

Here are a few practices you can implement immediately to begin systematizing your world:

1. **Automate What You Can**—In my household, milk, eggs, and bread are a necessity. Constantly needing to stop at the grocery store for replenishments became burdensome. I discovered a service that delivers groceries, so we decided to have them delivered to us instead of running out all the time for more. If you find something in your life that does not bring you joy, try to eliminate it through automation.

   I hate cleaning toilets and doing the laundry. So, I found a way to hire help for those chores. One benefit is that it makes us accountable for keeping the house clutter-free. The housekeepers can do their job well only if things are up off the floor and surfaces. Tuesday night in my house is "pickup time." The whole family gets involved to get the house ready. I realize housekeepers may not be in the budget for everyone, but if you can't yet afford one, you may be able to trade services with friends or come up with other creative solutions. One of my friends includes house cleaning as the exercise portion of the Life S.A.V.E.R.S., and a little gets done every morning.

2. **Briefcases and Beyond**—Hal, in addition to being a bestselling author, is also a speaker who travels week after week, sharing *The Miracle Morning* message with audiences around the world. Collecting the items he needed for every trip was time-consuming, inefficient, and ineffective, because he would often forget something at home or in his office. After the third time he forgot the charger for his computer and had to find an Apple store to buy a $99 replacement (ouch) or ask the front desk for a phone charger, shaver, or an extra set of cufflinks left behind by a previous guest, he'd had enough. He assembled a travel bag containing every item he

needs for his trips, and now he can leave at a moment's notice because his bag contains everything to conduct business on the road: business cards, brochures, copies of his books, adapters, and chargers for his phone and computer. He even includes earplugs in case his hotel room neighbor is noisy.

You'll know you need a system when you have a recurring challenge or find that you're missing important items because you're unprepared. If you're walking out the door with just enough time to get to your first destination of the day, only to discover your car is running on fumes, you need a system for getting out the door earlier. Here are some ways to plan ahead:

- Pack your lunch, your purse or briefcase, and your gym bag the night before, and also lay out your outfit for the next day.

- Prepare a bag with everything you need during your teaching day (pencils, erasers, paper, crayons, and lesson plans).

- Stash healthy snacks for when you're on the go (apples, kale chips, carrots, etc.) to prevent stopping at a convenience store or fast-food joint for a not-so-healthy option.

To put it another way: wherever you need to get your act together, you need a system. A life without systems is a life with unnecessary stress! This is especially true for busy teachers.

### 3. Foundational Scheduling

The use of a foundational schedule is key to maximizing your focus, productivity, and income. If we spend too many days bouncing around from one task to another and end far too many days wondering where the hell the time went and if any significant progress was made, we've missed more key opportunities than we can calculate. Can you relate?

I am going to share something with you that will transform your ability to produce consistent and spectacular results. *You must create a foundational schedule that gives structure and intentionality to your days and weeks.* A foundational schedule is a pre-determined, recurring schedule that is made up of focused time-blocks, which are each dedicated to your highest-priority activities. Most of us intuitively understand the benefits of scheduling, but very few do so effectively on a consistent basis.

I know, I know—you became an adult to get away from structure. Trust me, I get it. But the more you leverage a foundational schedule consisting of time-blocks—typically ranging from one to three hours each and dedicated to focusing on the projects or activities that will help you make the most of your life and business—the more freedom you'll ultimately create.

That's not to say you cannot have flexibility in your schedule. In fact, I strongly suggest that you *schedule* flexibility. Plan plenty of time-blocks for family, fun, and recreation into your calendar. You could even go as far as to include a "whatever I feel like" time-block, during which you do, well … whatever you feel like. You can also move things on occasion as needed. What's important is that you go through your days and weeks with a high level of clarity and intentionality with regards to how you're going to invest every hour of every day, even if that hour is spent doing *whatever you feel like*. At least you planned on it. Maintaining a foundational schedule is how you will ensure that you maximize your productivity, so that you almost never end the day wondering where in the hell your time went. It won't go anywhere without you making a conscious decision, because you'll be intentional with every minute of it.

I asked Hal to share his weekly foundational schedule so you can see an example of what this can look like. Although Hal has the luxury of entrepreneurial freedom and doesn't need to follow any pre-determined schedule, he will tell you that having this foundational schedule in place is one of his keys to ensuring he maximizes each day.

# Hal's Foundational Schedule

| TIME | MON | TUES | WED |
|------|-----|------|-----|
| 4:00 AM | SAVERS | SAVERS | SAVERS |
| 5:00 AM | Write | Write | Write |
| 6:00 AM | Emails | Emails | Emails |
| 7:00 AM | Take Kids to School | Take Kids to School | Take Kids to School |
| 8:00 AM | Team Mtg. | #1 Priority | #1 Priority |
| 9:00 AM | #1 Priority | Wakeboard | ↓ |
| 10:00 AM | ↓ | ↓ | ↓ |
| 11:00 AM | Lunch | Lunch | Lunch |
| 12:00 PM | Basketball | Priorities | Basketball |
| 1:00 PM | Priorities | Interview | Client Call |
| 2:00 PM | Priorities | Interview | Client Call |
| 3:00 PM | Priorities | Interview | Client Call |
| 4:00 PM | Priorities | Priorities | Priorities |
| 5:00 PM | FAMILY | FAMILY | FAMILY |
| 10:00 PM | Bed | Bed | Bed |

| TIME | THURS | FRI | SAT/SUN |
|---|---|---|---|
| 4:00 AM | SAVERS | SAVERS | SAVERS |
| 5:00 AM | Write | Write | Write |
| 6:00 AM | Emails | Emails | ⬇ |
| 7:00 AM | Take Kids to School | Take Kids to School | FAMILY Time |
| 8:00 AM | #1 Priority | #1 Priority | ⬇ |
| 9:00 AM | Wakeboard | ⬇ | ⬇ |
| 10:00 AM | ⬇ | ⬇ | ⬇ |
| 11:00 AM | Lunch | Lunch | ⬇ |
| 12:00 PM | Priorities | Basketball | ⬇ |
| 1:00 PM | Interview | Priorities | ⬇ |
| 2:00 PM | Interview | Priorities | ⬇ |
| 3:00 PM | Interview | Priorities | ⬇ |
| 4:00 PM | Priorities | PLANNING | ⬇ |
| 5:00 PM | FAMILY | Date Night | ⬇ |
| 10:00 PM | Bed | Bed | Bed |

(Note: Every hour is planned)

Keep in mind that, like most everyone, things come up that cause Hal's foundational schedule to change (events, speaking engagements, vacations, etc.), but only temporarily. As soon as he's back home and in his office, this is the schedule that he falls back into.

One of the main reasons that this technique is so effective is because it takes the emotional roller coaster out of decision-making for your daily activities. How many times has an appointment not gone well and that in turn affected your emotional state, and your ability to be productive, for the rest of the day? If you had followed a foundational schedule and the calendar told you your next activity was a networking event, writing ads, or making calls, you would have known what you needed to do next. If you remained committed to the calendar, then you would have had a fruitful afternoon.

Take control. Stop leaving your productivity up to chance and letting outside influences manage your calendar. Create your foundational schedule—one that incorporates everything you need to get done, as well as recreational, family, and fun time—and follow through with it, no matter what.

If you discover you need additional support to ensure that you keep to your plan, send a copy of your foundational schedule to an accountability partner or your coach, and have them hold you accountable. Your commitment to this one system will allow you to have significantly more control over your productivity and results.

## Principle #5: Commit to Consistency

If there is any not-so-obvious secret to success, this is it: *commit to consistency*. Every result that you desire—from improving your physique to improving your students' test scores to spending more quality time with your family—requires a consistent approach to produce the desired results.

In the chapters that follow, I'll give you the insight and direction you need to take consistent action. For now, prepare your mind to keep going—even when the results you want aren't coming fast enough. As you adjust to your new self, you'll have the stamina to withstand plenty of rejection and disappointment. The best teachers are consistent, persistent, and unfailing in their dedication to taking action every day, and you need to be the same!

## How is Your Self-Esteem Doing?

As American playwright August Wilson suggests, "Confront the dark parts of yourself, and work to banish them with illumination and forgiveness. Your willingness to wrestle with your demons will cause your angels to sing." Self-esteem gives you the courage to try new things and the power to believe in yourself.

It is vitally important that you give yourself permission to feel proud of yourself. Yes, we need to be realistic about our weaknesses and always strive to improve, but don't hesitate to be proud of your strengths and revel in the little wins. In the meantime, many days are filled with disappointments, delays, and denials, so it is vitally important that you love yourself. If you are doing the best you can, give yourself credit. I keep a special section in my journal to write love notes to myself. On days I need a little extra encouragement, I write down all the things I love and appreciate about me.

An unstoppable self-esteem is a powerful tool. You probably already know that if you have a negative attitude, you will go nowhere—and fast! With the right attitude, however, all the challenges of the day will roll off your back. You'll stay calm and keep going. When you are confident in your abilities and committed to consistency, your behavior will change, and your success is inevitable.

## Putting Self-Leadership into Action

Let's review the concepts we discussed in this chapter. We talked about the importance of self-leadership in improving your life, both personally and professionally. Developing self-leadership helps put you in the leadership role of your life. It eliminates the victim mentality and ensures you know the values, beliefs, and vision you want to live into.

**Step One:** Review and integrate the Five Foundational Principles of Self-Leadership:

1. **Take 100 Percent Responsibility.** Remember, the moment you accept responsibility for *everything* in your life is the moment you claim the power to change *anything* in your life. Your success is 100 percent up to you.

2. **Prioritize Fitness and Make Exercise Enjoyable.** If daily fitness isn't already a priority in your life, make it so. In addition to your morning exercise, block time for longer, thirty- to sixty-minute workouts three to five times each week. (If you're wondering which foods will give you a surplus of energy, we'll cover that in the next chapter.)

3. **Aim for Financial Freedom.** Begin to develop the mindset and habits that will inevitably lead you to a life of financial freedom, including saving a minimum of 10 percent of your income, continuously educating yourself on the topic of money, and diversifying your sources of income.

4. **Systematize Your World.** Start by creating a foundational schedule, and then identify which area(s) of your life or career can benefit by you putting systems and time-blocked schedules in place. When you predetermine your result-producing processes, your success is virtually guaranteed. Most importantly, make sure you instill a system for accountability into your world, whether that be working with a colleague or a coach or leveraging your colleagues and students by making commitments to them and leading by example.

5. **Commit to Consistency.** Everyone needs structure. Choose consistency and commit to personal expectations and values. If you're trying a new approach, give it an extended period to work before throwing in the towel.

**Step Two:** Develop your self-control and upgrade your self-image by using affirmations and visualization. Be sure to customize both at your earliest opportunity—it takes time to see results, and the sooner you start, the sooner you'll notice improvements.

By now, I hope you've gained a sense of how important your personal development is in creating success. As you continue to read this book—and I suggest you read it more than once—I recommend that you intentionally address the areas where you know you need improvement and expansion. If your self-esteem could use a boost, then take steps to elevate it. Design affirmations to increase and develop it over time. Visualize yourself acting with more confidence, raising your personal standards, and loving yourself more.

If this sounds overwhelming, remember the power of incremental change. You don't have to do everything all at once. And I've got more good news for you. In the next chapter, we're going to break down exactly how to engineer your life to create optimum levels of sustained physical, mental, and emotional energy, so that you're able to maintain extraordinary levels of clarity, focus, and action, day in and day out.

## Meet Legendary Teacher-Contributor
# Deanna Perkins
### Cedar Park, Texas, Second Grade

*The Miracle Morning* makes for more meaningful days. Samvi, age seven, walked into class one morning and said, "I woke up this morning, and I didn't want to come to school. But I thought about my affirmations, and it changed my mind. I am so happy to be here today, Mrs. Perkins."

My name is Deanna Perkins, and I'm a second-grade teacher in Cedar Park, Texas, USA. I've been teaching for fourteen years. Each year, I see a dip in self-confidence in my students. They come to class saying, "I'm not a good reader" or "I'm not good at math." I try to change this mindset as fast as I can.

I read *The Miracle Morning* in April of 2018 at my best friend Wendy's recommendation. I started waking up a little over an hour before my usual time to do my Life S.A.V.E.R.S. My children noticed a difference in my attitude and demeanor in the mornings and said they liked their mornings much better! I knew then that I should incorporate it with my students.

A week before officially starting the Life S.A.V.E.R.S. in class, I gave each child a spiral notebook to use for their *Miracle Morning*, and we set it up together. They wrote ten affirmations from a list of 101 kid-friendly positive thoughts. This made it easier for my seven- and eight-year-olds. We watched motivational videos. Instead of Life S.A.V.E.R.S., we do Life A.V.R.S.E.S. We always start our affirmations with our mantra, "Read it to believe it."

For visualization, they drew what they wanted in their future. It's incredible what these younger kids can think about their future! We also went digital; they created a vision board in Google Slides, and those turned out amazing!

Since there are different reading levels in my class, I allow students to choose a book for reading. Choice is important. They then go into scribing and journal about what comes to mind about themselves.

GoNoodle was the site of choice for our exercise. This site has many fun and silly dances for kids and "big kids" (a.k.a. we teachers who are young at heart).

When it came to meditation, this was (and still is) tough for some kids. The fact that they have to sit still, close their eyes, and focus on their breathing is a feat in itself. Using the Calm app, I use calming music, and I guide them on how to breathe ("Breathe in positivity, breathe out negativity" or "Breathe in growth mindset, breathe out fixed mindset"). They felt silly at first but quickly realized that it truly helped them to breathe and think positive. I also use meditation before times when I knew students would get anxious, such as before assessments.

The most important thing is what the kids think. Ainsley says, "My favorite part is meditation because it lets my calmness spread around." Hollis says, "My favorite part is the vision board because I get to draw what I want my future to be like." Samvi says, "I think it is awesome. It makes me ready for the day."

## Meet Legendary Teacher-Contributor
# Emily Schwepp
### First Grade

My name is Emily Schweppe, and I am a first-grade teacher in my fifth year of teaching. I came across the Miracle Morning Life S.A.V.E.R.S. in a Facebook group, and I immediately jumped at the opportunity to try it out in my classroom. Fostering social and emotional learning is a priority to me, so I knew the Miracle Morning would be a useful addition to my classroom.

My students were excited to begin the Miracle Morning! On the first day, we created a visual together for each of the Life S.A.V.E.R.S. that we then used every morning. In the beginning, students were having difficulty grasping the idea of setting a goal. One student said, "I want to play soccer in the fall!" and another said, "I want to play baseball in the summer!" While these are wonderful goals, I decided it would be better to discuss and then set short-term goals. By the end of the month, students were able to articulate their goals clearly: "I want to finish my practice packet!" or "I want to read two chapters of my book at home!" My favorite was Charles' goal, "I want to show sportsmanship in gym class today!"

The one minute of silence was a familiar activity, as we have been practicing mindful breathing throughout the year. Students enjoy our visual reminder of "smelling the flowers" and "blowing the bubbles" for mindful breathing.

I noticed the affirmations were uncomfortable for my students at first. We had a small discussion and then brainstormed a few general affirmations to choose from. After the second week, I knew my students became comfortable with the affirmations because they began to create different ones for themselves. Jason chose, "I'm a great skateboarder, I'm a great skateboarder," while Audrey's affirmation was, "I am positivity, I am positivity."

Similar to the affirmations, visualization was difficult for my students to understand in the beginning. I think this was tied to the lack of clarity with goal setting. I talked through the one minute of visualization as a reminder of what they were supposed to be visualizing.

During the one minute of reading, we used vocabulary words such as perseverance, empathy, or sportsmanship. I chose to do this because my students are familiar with these word cards and I have many developing readers, so I wanted to maintain a positive experience with the S.A.V.E.R.S.

My students declared that the writing was their favorite part and always wanted more time! Jacob drew a picture of himself showing his mom that he finished his chapter book with a conversation bubble saying, "Yes!"

Alison has asked that we continue with the S.A.V.E.R.S. because she loves writing about her goals!

When I begin this with my students next year, I will introduce each of the S.A.V.E.R.S. individually and spend a couple days practicing each one prior to putting it all together. We continue to enjoy those six miracle minutes each miracle morning!

# — 5 —

# NOT-SO-OBVIOUS LEGENDARY TEACHER PRINCIPLE #2:

## ENERGY ENGINEERING

*The world belongs to the energetic.*

—RALPH WALDO EMERSON

A s a teacher, you live and die by your own steam. Most of the time, if you don't have enough energy, you're not able to show up for your students as well as you could. The trouble is, it isn't all up to you. On some days—and I know you've had these days—you wake up, and you just don't have the energy or motivation you need to meet the inevitable challenges that you know are coming. Being a legendary teacher can be exhausting, both physically and mentally—and that's on the good days. To maintain your focus, amid uncertainty and overwhelm, is no easy task. The good days take energy, enthusiasm, and persistence. The hard days take all that and more.

Teaching *requires an abundance of energy*. There's no way around it. A teacher with low energy suffers greatly. Motivation is hard to sustain. Focus is often generated artificially by stimulants, such as almost every teacher's drug of choice—caffeine. You can have the best students, the best lesson plans, and the best action plan for the day, but if you don't have the *energy* to take advantage of them, reaching your goals is going to be unnecessarily difficult. If you want to maximize your effectiveness and really make a difference to your students, you need energy, lots and lots of energy—the more the better, and the more *consistent* the better.

- Energy is the fuel that enables you to maintain clarity, focus, and action, so that you can generate stellar results, day after day.

- Energy is contagious—it spreads from you to the world around you like a positivity virus, creating symptoms of enthusiasm and positive responses everywhere.

- Energy is the foundation of everything, and it is what determines the success we attract.

The question is, *how do you strategically engineer your life so that you maintain a high level of sustainable energy* that is always available to you on demand?

When we struggle with energy issues, we might try to compensate with caffeine and other stimulants, and they'll work for a while … until we crash. You may have noticed the same thing. You can lean on stimulants to build up energy for a short while, but then the energy seems to fall off just when you need it the most. Can't you just hear one of those infomercial hosts chime in here: *But there's got to be a better way!*

There is…

If you've been fueling yourself on coffee and pure determination, you haven't even begun to reach the heights of achievement that are possible when you understand how energy works and commit to engineering your life for optimum energy.

# Natural Energy Cycles

The first thing to understand about energy is that the goal isn't to be running at full speed all the time. Maintaining a constant output isn't practical. As human beings, we have a natural ebb and flow to our energy levels. Being the very best teacher you can be, it turns out, is the same. Know that you will need to access deeper wells of energy during particularly intense times throughout the year (standardized tests or finals, anyone?) and allow yourself the time to rest, rejuvenate, and recharge when the intensity lessens.

Just like houseplants need water, our energy reserves need regular replenishing. You can go full tilt for long periods of time, but eventually your mind, body, and spirit will need to be refilled. Think of your life as a container that holds your energy. When you don't properly manage what's in your container, it's like having a hole in the bottom. No matter how much you pour in, you still won't feel fully energized.

Instead of letting yourself get to the point of being overwhelmed, burned out, or stressed out, why not become proactive about your energy levels and have an auto-recharge system in place? This will help you plug the holes in your container and allow you to fill up with the energy you need.

If you have resigned yourself to being tired, cranky, behind on your to-do list, out of shape, and unhappy, I have some great news.

Being continually exhausted is not only unacceptable, *you don't have to settle for it.* There are a few simple ways to get what you need and want—more rest, time to replenish and recharge, and inner peace and happiness. A tall order? Yes. Impossible? Heck, no!

This is about strategically engineering your life for optimum and sustainable physical, mental, and emotional energy. Here are the three principles I follow to keep my energy reserves at maximum capacity and on tap for whenever I need them.

# 1. Eat and Drink for Energy

When it comes to energy engineering, what you eat and drink may play the most critical role of all. If you're like most people, you base your food choices on taste first and the consequences second (if you consider them at all). Yet, what pleases our taste buds in the moment doesn't always give us maximum energy to last throughout the day.

There is nothing wrong with eating foods that taste good, but if you want to be truly healthy and have the energy to perform like a champion, here's the big idea: it is crucial that we make a conscious decision to **place more value on the health and energy consequences of food than we do on the taste.** Why? Because digesting food is one of the most energy-draining processes that the body endures. Need evidence? Just take a second to think about how exhausted you feel after a big meal (see: Thanksgiving dinner). It's no coincidence that a large meal is usually followed by heavy eyes and ultimately a nap. They call it a "food coma" for a reason.

Foods like bread, cooked meats, dairy products, and any foods that have been processed require more energy to digest than they contribute to your body. So, rather than giving you energy, these essentially "dead" foods tend to drain your energy through digestion and leave you in an energy deficit. On the other hand, "living" foods like raw fruits, vegetables, nuts, and seeds typically give you more energy than they require for digestion, thus empowering your body and mind with an energy surplus, which enables you to perform at your best.

Put very simply, everything you put into your body either contributes to or detracts from your health and energy. Drinking water puts a check in the plus column; double shots of tequila won't. Eating a diet rich in fresh fruits and vegetables equals more plusses. Rolling through the drive-through to wolf down some fast food? Not so much. I know you know the drill. This isn't rocket science, but it may be the single most important area of your life to optimize. You may need to stop fooling yourself.

If you're not already doing so, it's time to be intentional and strategic about what you eat, when you eat, and—most importantly—*why* you eat, so that you can engineer your life for optimum energy.

## Strategic Eating

Up until this point, you may have been wondering, *when the heck do I eat during my Miracle Morning?* I'll cover that here. We'll also address *what* to eat for maximum energy, which is critical, and *why* what you choose to eat what you eat may be most important consideration of all.

**When to Eat:** Again, digesting food is one of the most energy-draining processes the body goes through each day. The bigger the meal and the more food you give your body to digest, the more drained you will feel. With that in mind, consider eating your first meal *after* your Miracle Morning. This ensures that, for optimum alertness and focus during the S.A.V.E.R.S., your blood will be flowing to your brain rather than to your stomach to digest your food.

However, I do recommend starting your day by ingesting a small amount of healthy fats as fuel for your brain. Studies show that keeping your mind sharp and your moods in balance may be largely related to the type of fat you eat. "Our brain is at least 60 percent fat, and it's composed of fats (like omega-3s) that must be obtained from the diet," says Amy Jamieson-Petonic, M.Ed., a registered dietitian, the director of wellness coaching at the Cleveland Clinic, and a national spokesperson for the American Dietetic Association.

After drinking his first full glass of water, Hal starts every morning with a tablespoon of organic coconut butter (specifically *Nutiva Organic Coconut Manna*, which you can order from Amazon.com) and a large mug of organic coffee, which he blends with Bulletproof Cacao Butter (available on Bulletproof.com). The tablespoon of coconut butter is such a small amount that it's easily digested, and it contains healthy fats to provide fuel for the brain. And the health benefits of cacao are significant, from being a powerhouse full of antioxidants (cacao rates in the top 20 on the oxygen radical absorbance capacity "ORAC" scale, which is used to rate the antioxidant capacity of foods) to lowering blood pressure.

Maybe most exciting is that eating cacao actually makes you happy! It contains phenylethylamine (known as the "love drug"), which is responsible for our state of mood and pleasure and the same feelings you get when you are in love. It also acts as a stimulant and can improve mental alertness. In other words, cacao equals win, win, win!

If you do feel like you must eat a meal first thing in the morning, make sure that it's a small, light, easily digestible meal, such as fresh fruit or a smoothie (more on that in a minute).

**Why to Eat:** Let's take a moment to delve deeper into *why* you choose to eat the foods that you do. When you're shopping at the grocery store, or selecting food from a menu at a restaurant, what criteria do you use to determine which foods you are going to put into your body? Are your choices based purely on taste? Texture? Convenience? Are they based on health? Energy? Dietary restrictions?

Most people eat the foods they do based mainly on the *taste* and, at a deeper level, based on our emotional attachment to the foods we like the taste of. If you were to ask someone, *"Why did you eat that ice cream? Why did you drink that soda?"* Or, *"Why did you bring that fried chicken home from the grocery store?"* You would most likely hear responses like, *"Mmm, because I love ice cream! ... I like drinking soda. ... I was in the mood for fried chicken."* All of these answers are based on emotional enjoyment derived primarily from the way these foods taste. In this case, this person is not likely to explain their food choices with how much value these foods will add to their health, or how much sustained energy they'll receive as a result of ingesting them.

My point is this: if we want to have more energy (which we all do) and if we want our lives to be healthy and disease-free (which we all do), then it is crucial that we reexamine why we eat the foods that we do. From this point forward—and I know we've covered this, but it bears repeating—*start placing significantly more value on the health and energy consequences of the foods you eat than you do on the taste.* The taste only provides you with a few minutes of pleasure, but the health and energy consequences impact the rest of your day and, ultimately, the rest of your life.

Again, in no way am I saying that we should eat foods that don't taste good in exchange for the health and energy benefits. I'm saying that we can have both. I'm saying that if we want to live every day with an abundance of energy so we can perform at our best and live long, healthy lives, we must choose to eat more foods that are good for our health and give us sustained energy, as well as taste great.

**What to Eat:** Before we talk about what to eat, let's take a second to talk about what to *drink*. Remember that Step #4 of the *5-Step Snooze-Proof Wake-Up Strategy* is to drink a full glass of water first thing in the morning so you can rehydrate and reenergize after a full night of sleep.

Next, like Hal, after I drink a full twenty-four ounces of water to rehydrate, I typically brew a pot of coffee. In fact, I set up my coffee during my nightly power-down ritual so it's ready to roll when I wake up. I usually wake up before my alarm, pop out of bed long enough to start the coffee, then meditate while it's brewing.

As for what to eat, it has been proven that a diet rich in *living foods*, such as fresh fruits and vegetables, will greatly increase your energy levels, improve your mental focus and emotional well-being, keep you healthy, and protect you from disease. So, Hal created the Miracle Morning Super-food Smoothie that incorporates everything your body needs in one tall, frosty glass! I'm talking about complete protein (*all* of the essential amino acids), age-defying antioxidants, omega-3 essential fatty acids (to boost immunity, cardiovascular health, and brain power), plus a rich spectrum of vitamins and minerals... and that's just for starters. I haven't even mentioned all the *super foods*, such as the stimulating, mood-lifting phytonutrients in cacao (the tropical bean from which chocolate is made), the long-lasting energy of maca (the Andean adaptogen revered for its hormone-balancing effects), and the immune-boosting nutrients and appetite-suppressing properties of Chia seeds.

The Miracle Morning Super-food Smoothie not only provides you with sustained energy, it also tastes great. You might even find that it enhances your ability to create miracles in your everyday life. You can download and print the recipe for free at www.TMMBook.com.

Remember the old saying *you are what you eat?* Take care of your body so your body will take care of you. You will feel vibrant energy and enhanced clarity immediately!

I have shifted my view of food from that of a reward, treat, or comfort, to that of fuel. I want to eat delicious, healthy foods that boost my energy levels and allow me to keep going as long as I need to go.

Don't get me wrong; I still enjoy certain foods that are not the healthiest choices, but I strategically reserve them for times when I don't need to maintain optimum energy levels, such as in the evenings and on weekends.

The easiest way for me to start making better decisions about my eating was to start paying attention to the way I felt after eating certain foods. I started setting a timer for sixty minutes after I finished each meal. One hour later, my timer went off, and I assessed my energy level. It didn't take long for me to recognize which foods gave me the biggest power boost and which ones didn't. I can clearly tell the difference in my energy level on the days when I drink a smoothie, or eat a salad, and the days I cave for a chicken sandwich or some of that pizza that smells so good. The former gives me a surplus of energy, while the latter puts me in an energy deficit.

What would it be like to give your body what it needs to work and play for as long as you'd like? What would it be like to give yourself exactly what you truly deserve? Give yourself the gift of great health, consciously chosen through what you eat and drink.

If you are eating throughout the day almost as an afterthought, maybe hitting a drive-through after you've hit the point of being famished, it is time to start building a new strategy.

Give some thought to the following:

• Can I start to consciously consider the consequences (both in health and energy) of what I eat and value those above the taste?

- Can I keep water with me so that I can hydrate with intention and purpose and avoid becoming dehydrated?

- Can I plan my meals in advance, including incorporating healthy snacks, so I can combat any patterns I have that don't serve me?

Yes, you can do all of these, and much more. Think about how much better your life will be and how much more energy you will have for your students when you become conscious and intentional about your eating and drinking habits.

- You will easily maintain a positive mental and emotional state. Low energy causes us to feel down, whereas high energy levels produce a positive state of mind, outlook, and attitude.

- You will be more disciplined. Low energy drains our willpower, making us more likely to choose doing the *easy* things over the *right* things. High energy levels increase our level of self-discipline.

- You will live longer.

- You will set an example for the people you lead and the people you love. How we live our lives gives permission to those around us to do the same.

- You will get healthier, feel much better, and live longer.

- Bonus—You will settle at your natural weight effortlessly.

- Best Bonus Ever—You'll be the best teacher you can be and impact your students at a higher level than ever before because you'll look and feel great!

Remember to stay hydrated throughout the day. Lack of water can lead to dehydration, a condition that occurs when you don't have enough water in your body to carry out normal functions. Even mild dehydration can drain your energy and make you tired.

By implementing the 5-Step Snooze-Proof Wake-Up Strategy, you'll have had your first glass of water at the start of the day. Beyond that, I recommend keeping a large water bottle with you and making a habit of drinking sixteen ounces every one to two hours. If remembering is a challenge for you, set a recurring timer or add multiple alarms on your phone to hold you accountable. Every time you hear a reminder, drink your water bottle, and refill it for the next round of rehydration. Keeping a full bottle with you will allow you to take in water as needed as well.

When it comes to frequency of eating, it's important to refuel every three to four hours, with small, easily digestible, living foods. My regular meals consist of some form of protein and vegetables. To keep my blood glucose levels from dropping, I snack frequently on living foods, including raw fruits and nuts, and one of my favorite go-to snacks—walnuts and a banana. I try to plan my best meals for the days I need to be the most productive.

I believe that eating for energy—from my first meal of the day until I'm done working—combined with exercise, gives me the freedom to eat what I want in the evenings and on weekends. I believe I can eat whatever I want, just not always as much as I'd like. I've learned to taste everything, but to eat just enough that I'm satisfied.

In the end, here is the simple thing to remember: food is fuel. We should use it to get us from the beginning of the day all the way to the end, while feeling great and having plenty of energy. Placing more value on the energy consequences of the foods you eat above the taste, as well as eating foods that fuel energy, is the first step in energy engineering.

## 2. Sleep and Wake to Win

*Sleep more to achieve more.* That might be the most counterintuitive productivity mantra you'll ever hear, but it's true. The body needs enough shut-eye each night to function properly and to recharge after a demanding day. Sleep also plays a critical role in immune function, metabolism, memory, learning, and other vital bodily functions. It's when the body does most of its repairing, healing, resting, and growing.

If you don't sleep enough, you're gradually wearing yourself down.

## Sleeping Versus Sleeping *Enough*

But how much is enough? There is a big difference between the amount of sleep you can get by on and the amount you need to function optimally. Researchers at the University of California, San Francisco, discovered that some people have a gene that enables them to do well on six hours of sleep a night. This gene, however, is very rare, appearing in less than 3 percent of the population. For the other 97 percent of us, six hours doesn't come close to cutting it. Just because you're able to function on five to six hours of sleep doesn't mean you wouldn't feel a lot better and get more done if you spent an extra hour or two in bed.

That may sound counterintuitive. I can almost hear you thinking, *spend more time in bed and get more done? How does that work?* But it has been well documented that enough sleep allows the body to function at higher levels of performance. You'll not only work better and faster, but your attitude will improve, too.

The amount of nightly rest each individual needs differs, but research shows that the average adult needs approximately seven to eight hours of sleep to restore the energy it takes to handle all of the demands of living each day.

Many of us have been conditioned to think we need eight to ten hours of sleep. In fact, sometimes we need less, and sometimes we need more. The best way to figure out if you're meeting your sleep needs is to evaluate how you feel as you go about your day. If you're logging enough hours, you'll feel energetic and alert all day long, from the moment you wake up until your regular bedtime. If you're not, you'll reach for caffeine or sugar mid-morning or mid-afternoon...or both.

If you're like most people, when you don't get enough rest, you have difficulty concentrating, thinking clearly, and even remembering things. You might notice your ineffectiveness or inefficiencies at home or at work, and you might even blame these missteps on your busy schedule. The more sleep you miss, the more pronounced your symptoms become.

In addition, a lack of rest and relaxation can really work a number on your mood. The classroom is no place for crankiness! It is a scientific fact that when individuals miss out on good nightly rest, their personalities are affected, and they are generally grumpier, less patient, and more likely to snap at people. The result of missing out on critical, much-needed rest might make you a bear to be around, which is not much fun for anyone, yourself included.

Most adults cut back on their sleep to pack more activities into their day. As you run against the clock to beat deadlines, you might be tempted to skimp on sleep in order to get more done. Unfortunately, lack of sleep can cause the body to run down, which allows illnesses, viruses, and diseases the tiny opening they need to attack the body. When you are sleep-deprived, your immune system can become compromised and is susceptible to just about anything. Eventually, lack of rest can cause illness that leads to missed days—or even weeks—of work. That's no way make a positive impact on the lives of your students.

On the flip side, when you get enough sleep, your body runs as it should, you're pleasant to be around, and your immune system is stronger. And that's precisely when you'll find yourself having more patience for your students and being able to tap into a deeper reserve of enthusiasm. Think of good sleep as the time when you turn on your inner magnet. Wake up rested and in a great mood because of your S.A.V.E.R.S., and you'll have better teaching days, because a happy teacher is also a fulfilled one.

## The True Benefits of Sleep

You may not realize how powerful sleep truly is. While you're happily wandering through your dreams, sleep is doing some hard work on your behalf and delivering a host of amazing benefits.

*Sleep improves your memory.* Your mind is surprisingly busy while you snooze. During sleep, you clean out damaging toxins that are byproducts of brain function during the day, along with strengthening memories and practicing skills learned while you were awake through a process called consolidation.

"If you are trying to learn something, whether it's physical or mental, you learn it to a certain point with practice," says Dr. David Rapoport, who is an associate professor at NYU Langone Medical Center and a sleep expert, "but something happens while you sleep that makes you learn it better."

In other words, if you're trying to learn something new, whether it's a foreign language, a new tennis swing, or the curriculum you're teaching, you'll perform better when you get adequate sleep.

*Sleep helps you live longer.* Too much or too little sleep is associated with a shorter life span, although it's not clear if it's a cause or an effect. In a 2010 study of women ages fifty to seventy-nine, more deaths occurred in women who got fewer than five hours or more than six-and-a-half hours of sleep per night. Getting the right amount of sleep is a good idea for your long-term health.

*Sleep fuels creativity.* Get a good night's sleep before getting out the easel and paintbrushes or the pen and paper. In addition to consolidating memories or making them stronger, your brain appears to reorganize and restructure them, which may result in more creativity as well.

Researchers at Harvard University and Boston College found that people seem to strengthen the emotional components of a memory during sleep, which may help spur the creative process.

*Sleep helps you attain and maintain a healthy weight more easily.* If you're overweight, you won't have the same energy levels as those at a healthy weight. If you are changing your lifestyle to include more exercise and diet changes, you'll want to plan an earlier bedtime. Putting additional physical demands on your body means you will need to counter-balance those demands with enough rest.

The good news: researchers at the University of Chicago found that dieters who were well-rested lost more fat—up to 56 percent more—than those who were sleep-deprived, who lost more muscle mass. Dieters in the study also felt hungrier when they got less sleep.

Sleep and metabolism are controlled by the same sectors of the brain, and when you are sleepy, certain hormones go up in your blood, and those same hormones drive appetite.

*Sleep lessens stress.* When it comes to our health, stress and sleep are closely connected, and both can affect cardiovascular health. Sleep can reduce stress levels, and with that comes better control of blood pressure. It is also believed that sleep affects cholesterol levels, which play a significant role in heart disease.

*Sleep helps you avoid mistakes and accidents.* The National Highway Traffic Safety Administration reported in 2009 that being tired accounted for the highest number of fatal, single-car, run-off-the-road crashes due to the driver's performance—even more than alcohol! Sleepiness is grossly underrated as a challenge by most people, but the cost to society is enormous. Lack of sleep affects reaction time and decision-making.

If insufficient sleep for only one night can be as detrimental to your driving ability as having an alcoholic drink, imagine how it affects your ability to maintain the focus necessary to become a tremendous teacher.

So, how many hours of sleep do you *really* need? You tell me, because only you truly know how much sleep you need to hit home run after home run. Now, if you really struggle with falling or staying asleep, and it is a concern for you, I highly recommend getting a copy of Shawn Stevenson's book, *Sleep Smarter: 21 Essential Strategies to Sleep Your Way to a Better Body, Better Health, and Bigger Success.* It's one of the best-written and most-researched books that I've seen on the topic of sleep.

Getting consistent and effective rest is as critical to performing at your best as what you do or don't have in your diet. A good night's sleep provides the basis for a day of clear thought, sustained energy, and peak performance. You probably already know how many hours you need to be at your best, and it's important that you are optimizing your sleep. However, what may be even more important than how many hours of sleep you get each night may be how you approach the act of waking up in the morning.

## You Snooze, You Lose: The Truth About Waking Up

The old saying, "you snooze, you lose" may have a much deeper meaning than any of us realized. When you hit the snooze button and delay waking up until you *have* to—meaning you wait until the time when you have to be somewhere, do something, or take care of someone else—consider that you're starting your day with resistance. Every time you hit the snooze button, you're in a state of resistance to your day, to your life, and to waking up and creating the life you say you want.

According to Robert S. Rosenberg, medical director of the Sleep Disorders Centers of Prescott Valley and Flagstaff, Arizona, "When you hit the snooze button repeatedly, you're doing two negative things to yourself. First, you're fragmenting what little extra sleep you're getting so it is of poor quality. Second, you're starting to put yourself through a new sleep cycle that you aren't giving yourself enough time to finish. This can result in persistent grogginess throughout the day." You can learn more about his work at http://www.answersforsleep.com.

If you're not already, make sure you start following the Five-Minute Snooze-Proof Wake-Up Strategy from Chapter 2, and you'll be poised to win. If getting to bed on time is your challenge, try setting a "bedtime alarm" that sounds an hour before your ideal bedtime, prompting you to start winding down so you can hit the sack.

On the other hand, when you wake up each day with passion and purpose, you join the small percentage of high-performing teachers who are living their dreams. Most importantly, you will be happy. By simply changing your approach to waking up in the morning, you will literally change everything. But don't take my word for it—trust these famous early risers: Oprah Winfrey, Tony Robbins, Bill Gates, Howard Schultz, Deepak Chopra, Wayne Dyer, Thomas Jefferson, Benjamin Franklin, Albert Einstein, Aristotle, and far too many more to list here.

No one ever taught us that by learning how to consciously set our intention to wake up each morning with a genuine desire—even enthusiasm—to do so, we can change our entire lives.

If you're just snoozing every day until the last possible moment before you have to head off to school or take care of your family, and then coming home and zoning out in front of the television until you go to bed, then *when are you going to develop yourself into the person you need to be to create the levels of health, wealth, happiness, success, and freedom that you truly want and deserve? When are you going to actually live your life instead of numbly going through the motions looking for every possible distraction to escape reality? What if your reality—your life—could finally be something that you can't wait to be conscious for?*

There is no better day than today for us to give up who we've been for who we can become and upgrade the life we've been living for the one we really want. There is no better book than the one you are holding in your hands to show you how to become the person you need to be, the one who is capable of quickly attracting, creating, and sustaining the life you have always wanted.

## How Much Sleep Do We *Really* Need?

The first thing experts will tell you is that there is no universal number of hours of sleep we need. The ideal duration of sleep varies from person to person and is influenced by factors such as age, genetics, stress, overall health, how much exercise a person gets, our diet—including how late we eat our last meal—and countless other factors.

For example, if your diet consists of fast food, processed foods, excessive sugar, etc., then your body will be challenged to recharge and rejuvenate while you sleep, as it will be working all night to detoxify and filter out the poisons that you've put into it. On the other hand, if you eat a clean diet made up of living food, as we covered in the last section, then your body will recharge and rejuvenate much more easily. The person who eats a clean diet will almost always wake feeling refreshed and with more energy, able to function optimally—even from less sleep—than the person who eats poorly.

According to the National Sleep Foundation, some research has found that long sleep durations (nine hours or more) are also associated with increased morbidity (illness, accidents) and even mortality (death). This research also found that variables such as depression were significantly associated with long sleep.

Since there is such a wide variety of opposing evidence from countless studies and experts, and since the amount of sleep needed varies from person to person, I'm not going to attempt to make a case that there is one right approach to sleep. Instead, I'll share Hal's own real-world results, from personal experience and experimentation, as well as from studying the sleep habits of some of the greatest minds in history. A small warning: some of this may be controversial.

## How To Wake Up With More Energy (On Less Sleep)

Through experimenting with various sleep durations—as well as learning those of many other Miracle Morning practitioners who have tested this theory—Hal made some startling discoveries. He found that our own personal *belief* about how much sleep we need affects our biology. In other words, how we feel when we wake up in the morning—and this is a very important distinction—is not solely based on how many hours of sleep we got, but how we told ourselves we were going to feel when we woke up.

For example, if you *believe* that you need eight hours of sleep to feel rested, but you're getting into bed at midnight and have to wake up at 6:00 a.m., you're likely to tell yourself, "Geez, I'm only going to get six hours of sleep tonight, but I need eight. I'm going to feel exhausted in the morning." Then, what happens as soon as your alarm clock goes off and you open your eyes and realize it's time to wake up? What's the first thought that you think? It's the same thought you had before bed! "Geez, I only got six hours of sleep. I feel exhausted." It's a self-fulfilling, self-sabotaging prophecy. If you tell yourself you're going to feel tired in the morning, then you are absolutely going to feel tired. If you believe that you need eight hours to feel rested, then you're not going to feel rested on anything less. But what if you changed your beliefs?

The mind-body connection is a powerful thing, and we must take responsibility for every aspect of our lives, including the power to wake up every day feeling energized, regardless of how many hours of sleep we get.

## 3. Rest to Recharge

The not-so-obvious counterpart to sleep is *rest*. While some people use the terms interchangeably, they're quite different. You might get eight hours of sleep, but if you spend all of your waking hours on the go, then you won't have any time to think or recharge your physical, mental, and emotional batteries. When you work all day, run from activity to activity after hours, and then finish with a quick dinner and a late bedtime, you don't allow for a period of rest.

Likewise, spending weekends taking the kids to soccer, volleyball, or basketball, then heading out to see a football game, going to church, singing in the choir, attending several birthday parties, etc., can do more harm than good. While each of these activities is great, maintaining a fully packed schedule doesn't allow for time to recharge.

We live in a culture that perpetuates the belief that when our days are busy and exciting, we are more valuable, more important, or more alive. In truth, we are all of those things when we can be at peace within our own skin. Despite our best intentions to live balanced lives, the modern world demands that we are almost always connected and productive, and these demands can drain us emotionally, spiritually, and physically.

What if, instead of being constantly on the go, you valued intentional quiet time, sacred space, and periods of purposeful silence? How might that improve your life, your physical and emotional well-being, and your ability to achieve success as a teacher?

It may seem counterintuitive to take time out when your to-do list is a mile long, but the fact is that more rest is a prerequisite to truly productive work.

Research proves that rest melts your stress away. Practices like yoga and meditation also lower heart rates, blood pressure, and oxygen consumption and alleviate hypertension, arthritis, insomnia, depression, infertility, cancer, and anxiety. The spiritual benefits of resting are profound as well. Slowing down and getting quiet means you can actually hear your own wisdom, your inner knowledge, and your inner voice. Rest and its close sibling, relaxation, allow us to reconnect with the world in and around us, inviting ease and a sense of contentment into our lives.

And yes, in case you're wondering, you'll be more productive, nicer to your friends and family members (not to mention your fellow teachers and your students), and in general much happier as well. When we rest, it's like letting the earth lie fallow rather than constantly planting and harvesting. Our personal batteries need to be recharged. The best way is to recharge them is to truly and simply rest.

## Easy Ways to Rest

Most of us confuse rest with recreation. To rest, we do things like hike, garden, work out, or even party. Any of these activities can only be termed restful because they are breaks from work, but truthfully, they are *not*, and *cannot*, be defined as rest.

Rest has been defined as a kind of waking sleep, experienced while you are alert and aware. Rest is the essential bridge to sleep, and we achieve rest and sleep the same way: by making space for them and allowing them to happen. Every living organism needs rest, including you. When we don't take the time to rest, eventually its absence takes a toll on the body. Here are ways to incorporate rest into your life:

- If you are not investing five or minutes each morning, during your S.A.V.E.R.S., to meditate or sit in silence, that is a great start.

- You can reserve Sundays or, if Sunday is a busy day for you, choose another day of the week for rest. You can read, watch a movie, do something low-key with family, or even spend time alone. Try cooking at home, playing games with your kids, and enjoying each other's (or your own) company.

- When you're driving, drive in silence: turn off the radio and stow your phone.

- Go for a walk without your earbuds in. Even a walk in nature without intention or goals, such as burning calories, can work.

- Turn off the television. Designate a half hour, an hour, or even half a day for silence. Try taking a few conscious breaths, during which you focus on the inhale and exhale or the space between breaths.

- You can also mindfully drink a cup of tea, read something inspirational, write in your journal, take a hot bath, or get a massage.

- Attend a retreat. It could be with your team, a group of friends, your church, any community with which you are involved, your family, your spouse, or yourself in nature.

Even taking a nap is a powerful way to rest and recharge. If I'm feeling drained during the day for some reason and still have a long day ahead, I won't hesitate to hit the reset button with a twenty- or thirty-minute power nap. Napping also can lead to better sleep patterns.

It's helpful to set a specific time for rest. Put boundaries around it so you can claim that time.

## The Rest Habit

As a teacher, you're in the trenches by default. You'll need to schedule your time for rest and self-care in the same way you schedule the other appointments in your life. The energy you get back will reward you many times over.

Rest certainly isn't something we were taught in school, and it may not come naturally at first. After all, you're a teacher, and teachers are always on the go and being of service to others. So, you may find that you need to consciously make it, and yourself, a priority. Learning different mindfulness practices and bringing them into your everyday life is an effective way to deeply rest your body, mind, and spirit. Practices such as mid-day meditation, yoga, and purposeful silence are powerful ways to go within and achieve restful states of being, particularly when you commit to practicing them regularly. And, as you'll learn later in this book, you have the opportunity to bring them into your classroom and model them for your students. What better way to influence the next generation than to show them how it's done?

The more you integrate periods of rest and silence into your daily life, the bigger the payoff will be. During more tranquil periods, perhaps you won't need to rest as much, but periods of intensity (such as during testing or just before school gets out for the summer) may require more rest and silence than usual.

Combining exercise, healthy food choices, consistent sleep, and rest will give you a quantum leap in the right direction for you and your business. Keep in mind that when you try to adopt these three practices—eating, sleeping, and resting more effectively—you may at first find adopting them to be uncomfortable. Your mind and body may encounter some emotional resistance. Resist the urge to run from the discomfort by making a commitment to begin putting them into practice, today.

## Putting Energy Engineering into Action

**Step One:** Commit to eating and drinking for energy by prioritizing the energy consequences of the foods you eat above the taste. After your initial glass of water in the morning, ingest some form of healthy fat to fuel your brain. Try incorporating one new healthy meal, made up of living foods, into your diet each day. Instead of snacking on potato chips, try kale chips, nuts, or fresh organic fruit. And remember to keep a full bottle of water with you all the time to stay hydrated.

**Step Two:** Sleep and wake to win by choosing a consistent daily bedtime and wake-up time. Based on what time you wake up to do your Miracle Morning, back your way into a bedtime that ensures you will get enough sleep. Maintain a specific bedtime for a few weeks to get your body acclimated. If you need a little nudge to get to bed on time, set a bedtime alarm that prompts you to start winding down one hour before bedtime. After a couple of weeks, feel free to play with the number of hours you leave for sleeping to optimize your energy levels.

**Step Three:** Incorporate time into your daily calendar to rest and recharge, whether that involves meditation, a nap, going for a walk, or doing an activity that brings you joy. Remember, Hal takes a two-hour lunch break every day, which gives him time to either play basketball or wakeboard—two activities that he loves to do and that thoroughly reenergize him. Which activities can you plan into your day that will reenergize you? In addition to your Miracle Morning routine, schedule regular daily periods to rest and recharge.

Now that you have a plan to take care of your body, in the next chapter we'll work on developing your unwavering focus.

## Meet Legendary Teacher-Contributor
# Jennifer Ozgur
### English Teacher, Twelfth Grade

I've been teaching middle and high school English for a suburban public school outside Philadelphia since 2000.

Since adopting the Life S.A.V.E.R.S. into my own life a few years ago, I've been wanting to incorporate the Miracle Morning into my classroom. A calm and centered student is more receptive to learning than one who feels anxious or distracted, and the Life S.A.V.E.R.S. are an excellent way to teach students successful strategies in a clear and deliberate way.

**HOW IT LOOKS IN MY CLASSROOM.** Just before class, I randomly distribute their journals with a daily one-page reading and suggested writing prompt, turn off the lights, and play relaxing music overhead and moving mandalas on the projection screen. Students come in, find their journals, and take a seat. After a few minutes, I invite them to read and then respond in their journals.

**WHAT TO EXPECT.** At first, some students mocked the process by snickering and chanting "Ohhhhmmmmmm..." in their best caricature of a yogi. I stayed patient, though, remembering that sometimes, the ones who fight it are the ones who need it the most.

Eventually, I noticed a shift in their behavior. For example, when students returned to school after a snow day, they were able to focus much better than anticipated because the Life S.A.V.E.R.S. routine anchored them and set the tone for our class. They'd enter, sit in their seats, close their eyes, take some deep breaths, and begin writing in their journals—quite a feat with a few inches of snow on the ground!

Other pleasant outcomes from using the Life S.A.V.E.R.S. were that I was a lot more relaxed as a teacher, and I found more of my students saying, "Hi, Mrs. Ozgur," in the hallways. Not only did it make a difference with the students, but it also added value to our student-teacher relationships.

**STUDENT FEEDBACK.** Most of my students (almost 90 percent) said they want to continue the Life S.A.V.E.R.S. routine. They said they like having a chance to collect their thoughts and process their day. Some said they noticed that they feel more in control of their lives, and their grades have been improving.

**TIPS:**

Select a purposeful time to roll out the Life S.A.V.E.R.S.: the beginning of the year, a new marking period, or concurrent with a new unit of study.

Be sure to give sufficient time to introduce the separate elements. The more they understand why they are so beneficial, the more likely they will embrace the practice. I allowed a full week to build up to the complete S.A.V.E.R.S. process, introducing a new letter each day. It took about two weeks to establish a routine, but it now runs like clockwork.

Give students opportunities for self-awareness, creating space for them to discover which approaches work best for them.

Model the practice, and, above all, relax and have fun!

## Meet Legendary Teacher-Contributor
# Jenn W.
### Teaching Fourth grade for Twenty-Three years, New Jersey

Our journey starts in my fourth-grade, urban, New Jersey classroom. My students come to school with different "baggage." Many have no encouragement or support at home. So, providing them with a personalized six- to ten-minute positive way to look at life played a major role in why I wanted to introduce them to the Miracle Morning. I not only teach them academics but need to provide opportunities to enhance their self-worth and encourage them to be productive members of our school, their family, and their community. Overexposure to a lot of negativity on television, the internet, and video games inspired me to incorporate this positive change. I knew from my own Life S.A.V.E.R.S. practice that this could help them, in some way, to start their day with a goal-oriented perspective and to create a more positive outlook.

I introduced the Miracle Morning Life S.A.V.E.R.S. practice by telling students about Hal's journey while stressing the importance of a positive way of seeing any situation with which they are faced.

Students kept a small journal to which they added an inspirational saying to the cover for affirmation. I explained the meaning of S.A.V.E.R.S., and we got started.

Beginning with guided silent time, students sat around the classroom, on rugs, under desks, or just at their seats. They enjoyed this time to reflect and calm down. I encouraged them to think of certain things or their favorite place, then to focus on breathing. Lastly, placing their hand on their heart, they thanked it for giving them life.

We recited affirmations or goals quietly. Some examples were: being a better goalie, getting a better grade in math, being a better friend, and doing homework every day.

Once affirmed, they closed their eyes and visualized how they would feel when their goal was reached. What would their parents say? The student who wanted to be a better goalie rejoiced one Monday morning, having saved three goals in her soccer game!

Exercising was most fun. Their goal was to move continuously for one minute. Though challenging at first, the more we did it, the more determined they became, and it really got them motivated to learn. They discovered creative ways to keep moving: dances, jumping jacks, and just fun movement. I found that this also benefited them during other low times during the day, and a few students tried it at home while they watched television or played video games.

Reading involved one-page stories with a positive message. Some favorites included "The Lion and the Mouse," "The Laughter Box," and "The Frog Race." We discussed the lesson revealed and how to incorporate them in our everyday interactions.

Scribing allowed time to reflect on their reading or any thoughts about the S.A.V.E.R.S. experience. One student wrote: "I would like to spend more time with my family instead of video games," and another, "Doing S.A.V.E.R.S. in the morning really helps me to relax."

Inspiring challenged children to be positive and accountable with the right tools, and the Miracle Morning Life S.A.V.E.R.S., makes this extremely worthwhile.

# — 6 —

# NOT-SO-OBVIOUS LEGENDARY TEACHER PRINCIPLE #3:

## UNWAVERING FOCUS

*The successful warrior is the average man, with laser-like focus.*

—BRUCE LEE, WORLD-RENOWNED
MARTIAL ARTIST AND ACTOR

We've all met that person. You know—*that* person. The one who runs marathons, coaches little league, volunteers at her son's school lunch program, is an incredible parent, and maybe writes a novel on the side. And on top of all that? She's an incredible teacher, getting tons of recognition for her teaching skills, winning awards, and knocking it out of the park when it comes to educating her students, year after year. I bet you know someone like that—someone who just seems inexplicably productive.

Or maybe you know *this* person—the teacher who teaches by day and tutors by night, while still spending ample time with his family; does his daily 5 a.m. CrossFit workout; and tells you about the latest novel he read. He's fit, always happy, and makes every person he encounters feel like a million bucks.

What you might not realize, though, is exactly how they do it. Maybe you always thought they were lucky. Or gifted. Or connected. Or had the right personality. Or were independently wealthy. Or born with superpowers!

While those things can help when it comes to teaching, I know from experience that the real superpower behind every unbelievably productive person is *unwavering focus*. Unwavering focus is the ability to maintain clarity about your highest priorities, while taking all the energy you've learned to generate for yourself, channeling it into what matters most, and keeping it there, regardless of what is going on around you or how you feel. This ability is key to becoming a legendary teacher.

When you harness the power of focus, you don't become superhuman, but you can achieve seemingly superhuman results. And the reasons for this are surprisingly straightforward.

Unwavering focus makes you more effective. Being effective doesn't mean doing the most things or doing things the fastest. It means doing the right things. You engage in the activities that create forward momentum toward your life's goals.

- **Unwavering focus makes you more efficient.** Being efficient means doing things with the fewest resources, such as time, energy, or money. Every time your mind wanders away from your goals, you waste those things—particularly time. In pursuit of our goals, time is always in demand, so every moment that your focus wavers is another moment lost.

- **Unwavering focus makes you productive.** Understand that just because you're *busy* does not mean you're productive. In fact, struggling teachers are usually the busiest. Too often we confuse being busy—engaged in activities that don't produce results, like checking emails or cleaning your car or reorganizing your to-do list for the twelfth time this month—with being productive. When you have a clear vision, identify your highest priorities, and consistently execute your most leveraged activities, you'll go from being busy to being productive. By taking the steps that we're about to cover, you'll learn how to develop the habit of unwavering focus and join the ranks of the most productive people in the world.

• If you combine those benefits, you will achieve *a lot* more. Perhaps the greatest value of focus, however, is that rather than scattering your energy across multiple areas of your life and getting mediocre results across the board, you will release untapped potential *and* improve your life.

Now let's turn your Miracle Morning to the task. Here are four steps you need to take to follow up your Miracle Morning with sustained focus.

## 1. Create Your Best Environment(s) for Unwavering Focus.

Let's start here: *you need a teaching environment that supports your commitment to unwavering focus.* A classroom that is designed in a way that supports you is crucial to your teaching success and happiness. A desk and even larger workspace that are carefully and thoughtfully organized will all but ensure you will complete all necessary tasks and in record time. A "home base" for your work will support your goals and objectives in ways you may not have imagined.

Part of the reason for this is simple logistics. If your materials are scattered from the trunk of your car to your desk and then to the kitchen counter, you can't be effective. A bigger reason, however, is that **having a place where you focus will trigger the habit of focusing**. Sit at the same desk to do great work at the same time every day, and soon enough you'll find yourself slipping into the zone just by sitting down in that chair.

Because you have many others coming in and out of your space regularly, putting your workspace and materials in order will minimize the amount of time you are off-task and unfocused when you are interrupted. When you are prepared and always have exactly what you need at your fingertips, you can handle disruptions in stride.

## 2. Clear the Unfocused Clutter.

Clutter is a focus killer, and it's our next stop on the journey. There is a reason that Marie Kondō's book, *The Life-Changing Magic of Tidying Up*, is one of the best-selling non-fiction books of the last decade and has even inspired a Netflix series! When you declutter both your physical and mental space, a calm, motivated mindset will make way for inspiration and effortless productivity.

There are two kinds of clutter, mental and physical, and we all have them both. We carry around thoughts in our minds like these: *My sister's birthday is coming up. I should get her a gift and card. I had a great time at dinner the other night. I need to send the host a thank-you note. I must answer the email from my new client before I leave the office today.*

Then there are the physical items we accumulate: stacks of paper, old magazines, sticky notes, clothes we never wear, the pile of junk in the garage. The trinkets, knick-knacks, and tokens that accumulate as we go through life. Not to mention graded tests, completed projects, and stacks of assignments.

Clutter of either type creates the equivalent of a heavy fog, and to become focused, you need to be able to *see*. To clear your vision, you'll want to get those mental items out of your head and collected so you can relieve the mental stress of trying to remember them. And then, you'll want to get those physical items out of your way.

Here's a simple process to help you clear the fog and create the clarity you need to focus. And yes, do this for both your home and classroom!

- **Create a master to-do list.** You probably have lots of to-do items you haven't even written down yet; start with those. Add the contents of all those sticky notes that clutter your desk, computer screen, planner, countertops, and refrigerator (are there other places?). Put those notes and action items on your master list in one central location, whether that's a physical journal or a list on your phone, so that you can clear your mental storage. Feeling better? Keep going; we're just getting started.

- **Purge your workspace(s).** Schedule one or two half (or full) days to go through every stack of paper, file folder stuffed with documents, and tray full of unopened mail—you get the gist. Throw out or shred what you don't need. Scan or file the papers and documents that matter. Note in your journal any items that need your attention and cannot be delegated, then schedule a time to complete them.

- **Declutter your life.** Wherever possible, clean up and clear out every drawer, closet, cabinet, and trunk that doesn't give you a sense of calm and peace when you see it. This includes your car. This might take a few hours or a few days. Schedule a short time each day until everything is complete. Saying, "I just need a weekend to declutter," is a sure way to never start. Pick a single drawer and start there. You'll be surprised at how the little bursts of work accumulate. Try S.J. Scott and Barrie Davenport's book, *10-Minute Declutter: The Stress-Free Habit for Simplifying Your Home* for suggestions.

Getting physically and mentally organized will allow you to focus at a level you would never believe possible. It leaves your energy nowhere to go except to what *matters*. It is easy to dismiss or downplay the power of clean, organized spaces, but it is with absolute conviction I tell you not to! When everything has a place and is in its place, you will benefit in ways you can't yet imagine.

# 3: Protect Yourself from Interruptions.

In addition to my core businesses, I am writing this book and am married with one daughter and three furry children. As you can imagine, my time is critically important to me, just as I'm sure yours is to you.

To avoid distraction and ensure that my attention is focused on the task at hand, my phone is almost always set on Do Not Disturb mode. This blocks all incoming calls, texts, or notifications like email and social media. This is a simple thing that dramatically increases my daily productivity and ability to remain focused on the task at hand. I recommend returning phone calls and emails at pre-designated times according to your schedule, not everybody else's.

You have the added reason to not entertain interruptions: you're teaching! Unless someone has a terrific reason, or a true emergency, they expect you simply can't be disturbed. Take advantage of this natural boundary and extend it to suit your goals.

Additionally, you can apply the same philosophy and strategies to any notifications and/or alerts, as well as your availability for colleagues, friends and family, and even, yes, the school administration. Do Not Disturb isn't just a setting on your phone. Let everyone important to you know when you're available and when they need to leave you undisturbed. You might just be surprised at how willing they are to support you.

## 4. Build a Foundation for Unwavering Focus.

Once you identify your focus place and begin the process of decluttering your life, you should experience a remarkable increase in focus simply from clearing the fog in your mind.

Now, it's time to take things to the next level. I use three questions to improve my focus:

- What's working that I should *keep doing* (or do more of)?
- What do I need to *start doing* to accelerate results?
- What do I need to *stop doing* immediately that's holding me back from going to the next level?

If you can answer those three questions and act on the answers, you'll discover a whole new level of productivity you probably didn't think was possible. Let's look at each question in detail.

### What Do You Need to *Keep Doing* (or Do More of)?

Let's face it, not all tactics and strategies are created equal. Some work better than others. Some work for a while and then become less effective. Some even make things worse.

Right now, you're probably doing a lot of the right activities, and you'll be nodding right along as you read the coming chapters on the ABCs of being a phenomenal teacher. If you already know the things you're doing that are working, jot those down. Perhaps you're already using the Do Not Disturb function, or you're already well into a fitness challenge and feeling stronger each day, for example. Put that on the "what's working" list.

Make sure you're choosing things that contribute to increasing your success, and the success of your students, as a whole. It's easy to keep the things you *like* doing, but you need to make sure that the activities you're doing are directly related to becoming more successful. Consider the 80/20 Rule (known as the Pareto Principle), which shows that roughly 80 percent of our results come from 20 percent of our efforts. Which 20 percent of your activities impact 80 percent of your results? It's easy to keep the things that you *like* doing, but this is reality—you need to make sure that the activities you're doing are directly related to the business at hand, as well as advancing your teaching career.

At the end of this chapter, you'll have an opportunity to capture in your journal the activities that are working. (Among them, hopefully, will be that you've started doing the Life S.A.V.E.R.S.) Everything that's on that list is a "keep doing" task until it's replaced by something even more effective.

For each of the "keep doing" activities on your list, make sure you're completely honest with yourself about *what you need to be doing more of* (in other words, what you're currently not doing enough of). If it's something you think you should be doing, such as taking on additional classes or designing an improved curriculum, but it's not moving you forward toward your important goals, it doesn't belong on your list. Perfection is not one of the goals here. Overworking yourself is ultimately unproductive and takes your focus off the important things.

Keep doing what's working, and, depending on how much more you want to achieve, simply do *more* of what's working.

## What Do You Need to *Start* Doing?

Once you've captured what's working and determined what you need to do more of, it's time to decide what else you can do to accelerate your success.

I have a few top-shelf suggestions to prime the pump and get you started:

- Read a book every week on one of your subjects to increase your knowledge base.

- Get to school fifteen to thirty minutes earlier so you can enjoy some quiet time before the first students arrive.

- Schedule time on Friday afternoons before leaving school to finalize lesson plans for the following week.

- Conduct weekly meetings and/or put together a book club with some of your fellow teachers who are also practicing the Life S.A.V.E.R.S.

- Perform cleanup time every day.

- Create your foundational schedule—the recurring, ideal weekly schedule with a time-blocked calendar mentioned previously—so that every day when you wake up, your highest priorities are already predetermined and planned. Then, make any necessary adjustments on Sunday night for the following week.

- Have whatever teaching tools and materials you might need on hand at all times. Be sure to stock and re-stock so you are always prepared.

I caution you to not become overwhelmed here. Keep in mind that Rome wasn't built in a day. You don't need to identify fifty-eight action items and implement them by tomorrow. The great thing about having a daily scribing practice as part of your Miracle Morning means you can capture everything that needs to be done. Then add them, one or two at a time, to your success toolbox until they become habits. Incremental improvements have a magical way of accumulating.

# What Do You Need to *Stop* Doing?

By now, you've most likely added a few items to start doing. If you're wondering where the time is going to come from, this might be your favorite step of all. It's time to let go of the things you've been doing that don't serve you to make room for the ones that do.

I'm fairly sure you do a number of daily activities you will be relieved to stop doing, thankful to delegate to someone else or grateful to just release.

Why not stop:

- eating unhealthy, energy-draining foods that suck the life and motivation out of you?
- doing unnecessary household chores?
- replying to texts and emails instantly?
- answering the phone? (Let it go to voicemail and reply when the timing works best for you.)
- reading and posting on social media sites?
- watching hours of television every day?
- beating yourself up or worrying about what you can't change?
- doing repetitive tasks such as paying the bills, buying groceries several times a week, or even cleaning your house?

Or, if you want to improve your focus dramatically in one simple step, try this easy fix: *stop responding to buzzes and sounds like a trained seal.*

Do you really need to be alerted when you receive texts, emails, and social media notifications? Nope, didn't think so. Go into the settings of your phone, tablet, and computer, and turn all your notifications OFF.

Technology exists for your benefit, and you can take control of it this very minute. How often you check your phone messages, texts, and email can and should be decided by you. Let's face it, teaching is not a job that will result in a life-or-death situation if you do not respond immediately to a call, text, or email. We don't need to be accessible 24/7/365 except to our significant others and our children. An effective alternative is to schedule times during the day to check on what's happening, what needs your immediate attention, what items can be added to your schedule or master to-do list, and what can be deleted, ignored, or forgotten.

## Final Thoughts on Unwavering Focus

Focus is like a muscle that you build over time. And, like a muscle, you need to show up and do the work to make it grow. Cut yourself some slack if you falter, but keep pushing forward. It will get easier. It might take you time to learn to focus, but every day that you try, you'll continue to get better at it. Ultimately, this is about *becoming* someone who focuses, which starts with seeing yourself as such. I recommend that you add a few lines to your affirmations about your commitment to unwavering focus and what you will do each day to develop it.

Most teachers would be shocked to discover just how little time they spend on truly important and relevant activities each day. Today, or in the next twenty-four hours, schedule sixty minutes to focus on the *single most important task you do*, and you'll be amazed by not only your productivity but also how empowering it feels.

By now, you've added some pretty incredible action items and focus areas to your success arsenal. After you complete the steps below, head into the next section where we will sharpen your teaching skills and combine them with the Life S.A.V.E.R.S. in ways you might not have heard or thought of before! Remember the steps we discussed in this chapter on the importance of unwavering focus and the ways to increase it in your life.

## Putting Unwavering Focus into Action

**Step One:** Choose or create your ideal environment(s) to support unwavering focus. If your focus is optimum when you're working in the Teacher's Lounge after hours, schedule focused time-blocks there. If you bring work home to do, make sure you've implemented step two, below.

**Step Two:** Clear your physical and mental clutter. Start by scheduling a half day to clean up your workspace. Then, clear your mind with a brain dump. Unload all those little to-do lists floating around in your head. Create a master to-do list on your computer, in your phone, or in your journal.

**Step Three:** Protect yourself from interruptions by turning off notifications and by putting your phone into Do Not Disturb mode, and ask your circle of influence to leave you alone during your focused time-blocks.

**Step Four:** Start building your unwavering focus lists. Pull out your journal, or open a note on your phone or computer, and create the following three lists:

- **What I need to keep doing (or do more of)?**
- **What I need to start doing?**
- **What I need to stop doing?**

Begin jotting down everything that comes to mind. Review your lists, and determine which activities could be automated, outsourced, or delegated. How much time do you spend on your most important activities? Repeat this process until you are clear on what your process is, and start time-blocking your days so that you're spending close to 80 percent of your time on tasks that produce results. Delegate the rest.

You've now got a great handle on how to incorporate the Life S.A.V.E.R.S. into your work and personal life. It's time to go deeper into the skills that make a teacher legendary in every way. When you're ready, let's begin.

## Meet Legendary Teacher-Contributor
# Julie Ornelas
### Visual Arts Teacher, Oak Ridge High School

I teach visual arts to ninth through twelfth graders at a high school in Northern California. I teach because I care deeply about connecting with students and allowing them to find their voices, to be their truest selves, and to create their own happiness. These passions have been enhanced by my experience with *The Miracle Morning*.

I learned about *The Miracle Morning* several years ago while listening to a podcast interview with Hal Elrod. Hal's story was moving and inspiring. I immediately purchased his book and started practicing the Life S.A.V.E.R.S. as part of my daily routine. Practicing Life S.A.V.E.R.S. gave me focus and motivation to propel me toward my goals. Over time, pieces of the program found their way into my classroom. I started with scribing. My students start every class by writing or drawing what they are grateful for, looking forward to, or excited about in their artist's journals. After scribing, students share these "good things" with their classmates. Next, I added a minute of silent breath-body awareness to the beginning of each period, providing us with time to relax and focus inward.

When I discovered Hal and Honorée were writing *The Miracle Morning for Teachers*, I embraced the opportunity to pilot the program in its entirety, because I knew my students would benefit tremendously. To kick off, I told my students about Hal and his amazing story. I asked students to choose a goal they felt passionate about. Students used mixed media to create visual representations of their goals and affirmations in their journals. These artworks became our focus for the visualization and affirmation portions of the Life S.A.V.E.R.S. Our minute of silence easily led to a guided visualization of our goals and affirmations. For the reading, I picked quotes from famous artists. Our minute of exercise usually took the form of stretching, chair yoga, or standing poses. After getting into the swing of things, I had students lead the exercise portion of the routine.

After the first day of sharing my personal goals and affirmations with each of my classes, I noticed myself repeating my affirmation like a mantra. Never before had I experienced an affirmation taking hold quite so profoundly. I believed what I was telling myself and knew my students would believe in themselves too. As we focused on our goals as a class, our discussion of good things became more personal and meaningful, connecting us as a classroom community on a deeper, more intimate level. The power of the Life S.A.V.E.R.S. was taking hold in more ways than I had expected, and we had only just begun.

This year, I have seen my students grow in unexpected ways. Students who were not engaged discovered the tools they needed to motivate themselves to achieve their goals. My students reported experiencing less stress and increased motivation, focus, and sense of purpose. I look forward to starting a new school year with the Life S.A.V.E.R.S., setting goals with a new set of students, and seeing where the Miracle Morning will take us.

## Meet Legendary Teacher-Contributor
# Kathy Jardine
### Durand High School, Durand, Wisconsin

My name is Kathy Jardine, and I currently teach high school science in a rural district in Durand, Wisconsin. I read Hal Elrod's book, *The Miracle Morning*, and incorporated it into my life. The students who participated in my classroom Miracle Morning experiment were seventeen to eighteen years old.

I truly believe mindfulness is important in the technology-induced, busy lifestyle in which we so often choose to partake. Therefore, I wanted to share these ideas with my students to help them realize the importance of setting and visualizing goals, learning to be mindful, stating positive affirmations, and changing how they think in only six minutes per day. I knew that if they could experience these concepts, they would also enjoy the benefits from them.

To begin implementation in my classroom, I typed up an instruction sheet as to what we would be doing every day, along with a journal sheet for each student. Students wrote their own goal, and I walked them through each part of the routine. Daily, we did each activity at the start of class in the order provided. The majority of the class said they loved the Silence, and some students even asked if the time could be extended two to three minutes. Sue said, "The breathing/resting exercises helped me feel better about each class period. I was able to take a minute to clear my mind before class." Alex added, "I was able to relax, without thinking about anything. It was so refreshing because I have never done this before. I even found myself doing it at home. It really helps me." Affirmations, Visualization, and Scribing provided similar positive feedback. According to Sam, "The affirmations and the visualization helped me in my life. I always think about things I want to accomplish, but I have never written them down. This forced me to actually think deeper about them."

While most of the activities had positive feedback, Exercise and Reading didn't as much. Students did not want to exercise, and several stated that it gave them anxiety and stressed them out due to concerns over what others thought or how they would look. Being teenagers who are still learning who they are, I completely understood this. Therefore, I switched from exercise to stretching, and they were more responsive to this. Additionally, the reading portion was hard for most students as well. The majority commented that one minute was simply too short of a time frame, as it took longer than that for students to locate their reading material and find where they left off.

I did notice an overall calming effect in my classroom each day, and I will continue the process in the future with a few changes. I will start with stretching, and, when students are comfortable with each other, I might switch to exercise. Unfortunately, I am not sure I will include the reading portion at all. Even with these changes, I still feel students will receive the full benefits of the process.

I am grateful for this opportunity, along with the knowledge and tools I have gained in this process. Thank you!

# SECTION 3:

# THE ABC'S OF BEING
# A LEGENDARY TEACHER

# — 7 —
# LEGENDARY TEACHER SKILL #1:
## A+ ATTITUDE OPTIMIZATION

*People may hear your words, but they feel your attitude.*

–JOHN C. MAXWELL

No person on the planet has better displayed the power of a positive attitude than Hal. At age twenty, when his Ford Mustang was struck head-on by a drunk driver who was traveling at over seventy miles per hour, Hal was found dead at the scene. His heart stopped beating for six minutes. He then spent the next six days in a coma, flat-lining twice more during that time. When he woke from the coma, his parents and doctors informed Hal that he had died for six minutes, broken eleven bones, suffered permanent brain damage and would likely never walk again.

Presented with this devastating news and facing an unimaginable reality, how did Hal respond? He told his parents that if the doctors were correct, and he was to spend the rest of his life in a wheelchair, unable to walk, he had already decided that he would consciously choose to be the happiest and most grateful person one had ever seen in a wheelchair. He explained that he would never let his circumstances determine his emotional well-being and quality of life. Doctors thought he was in denial, and possibly delusional, but he wasn't. In fact, three weeks after he was found dead, he took his first step, demonstrating the nearly limitless impact that our attitude can have in our lives. But that was only the beginning.

At age twenty-six, during the economic collapse of 2008, Hal experienced what he refers to as his second "rock bottom." When the economy crashed, so did he. His business failed, his home was foreclosed on by the bank, his body fat percentage tripled, and he plummeted deep into debt and became deeply depressed. However, he also accepted total responsibility for managing his attitude and turning his life around. He developed a daily morning ritual made up of the six most timeless and proven personal development practices known to man (which eventually became the Life S.A.V.E.R.S.), and committed to helping others by sharing his newfound ritual in a book titled, *The Miracle Morning*. Little did he know that his taking responsibility for optimizing his attitude would impact the lives of millions of people.

Fast forward to age thirty-seven (just two years before this book was written), and the worst was yet to come. Married to the woman of his dreams and a father of two young children, Hal was diagnosed with a rare and aggressive form of cancer (acute lymphoblastic leukemia) and given a grim 30 percent chance of surviving. Faced with the statistical probability of dying, leaving his wife without a husband and their children without a father, how did he respond? The day he was diagnosed, Hal reassured his wife, Ursula, "Sweetheart, I know this is scary, and I'm not going to sugarcoat it—this will probably be the most difficult thing our family has ever endured— but I also have unwavering faith that it will also be the *best* thing that has ever happened to me, and for our family. And just like with my car accident, I promise you I will be the happiest and the most grateful I've ever been *while* I'm enduring what will likely be the most difficult time in my life."

After surviving what has indeed proven to be the most difficult couple of years of his life, I'm grateful to report that Hal is now in remission (a.k.a. cancer-free) and furthering his mission to elevate the consciousness of humanity, one person at a time. He will be the first to tell you, "Your quality of life has little to do with what's going on *around* you, and everything to do with what's going on *inside* of you. In other words, more than anything else, your quality of life—and the quality of your relationships, both personally and professionally—is determined by your attitude. Thus, learning how to optimize your attitude may be the most important skill you can commit to mastering."

To have a positive, lasting impact on your students, it will come as no surprise that optimizing your attitude—an A+ Attitude—will make having that impact easier. It also will make you more effective in every way.

You can develop your A+ Attitude right in conjunction with your Life S.A.V.E.R.S. As you do, you'll enjoy teaching even more than ever before—and watch the ripple effect happen right before your very eyes. Just imagine the impact that sharing these transformative tools will have on your students a month, a school year, even a decade from now, and the ongoing impact it will have on the people around them.

Your Life S.A.V.E.R.S. practice will go a long way toward optimizing your attitude, but we know teachers have to be prepared for just about anything. Having an A+ Attitude will ensure you are prepared for and can weather any storm that comes your way.

The ABCs of developing an A+ Attitude are *approach, belief,* and *character*. To make the most direct and meaningful impact on your students, it is helpful to not only know them, but to commit to mastering them. And this chapter is going to help you do just that!

Attitudes are, as they say, contagious. We want to help you ensure that yours is worth catching!

# Attitude Sub-Skill #1: Approach—*to come near in character, time, amount, etc.*

How you approach your day, your classroom, and your students will directly impact their experience, how well they learn, and how much they learn and retain.

In a previous life, I was a successful network marketer. My mentor and direct upline used to say, "Catch yourself on fire and people will come for miles around to watch you burn." Obviously, "fires" and "classrooms" don't go together, but I'm sure you get my gist. It is no surprise, then, that if you're "on fire" (i.e. positive, enthusiastic, and fun!) for your students and your subject(s), they are going to be more open and receptive to each and every message that you to deliver to them.

Before you ever see another human on any given day, don't you owe it to them (and yourself) to put yourself in a positive space? To be in the best mood you can be? The answer to both of those questions is a resounding *yes*.

Creating a positive environment in your classroom will, by default, ensure both you and your students are able to thrive. Building a community within the classroom will allow each child to feel known, safe, and valued. And those are simply the basics. Your A+ Attitude optimization will also create an encouraging, can-do setting in which your students feel empowered to do anything— including learn not just your curriculum but also the intangible takeaways that you embody, which will serve them well throughout their lives.

Here are a few practices you can add to optimize how you approach each day:

- Smile! A cornerstone of your A+ Attitude is making sure your face conveys how happy you are to see your students. Although this may seem obvious, it's crucially important and often requires being intentional as your students enter your classroom.

- Make your classroom feel "happy." Open the blinds or shades, hang posters with positive messages (or make your own), and even consider playing upbeat, positive music as your students come into class. If you can paint, paint! There is a whole science of color, and you can use color to invoke joy, happiness, and positive energy.

- Find a silver lining. If (when!) something goes wrong, find and focus on the positive. Be a good finder, and teach your students to be good finders, too.

- Sprinkle compliments like confetti. I once saw a quote that read, "Be mindful of what you say to children, because your words become their inner voice." No matter one's age, what others say to us affects our self-esteem, and teachers have the opportunity to speak life, belief, and confidence into their students. When you compliment their outfit or the sticker on their binder, they know they are seen. When you catch them doing something right and articulate it, you reinforce their positive behavior and unconsciously give them permission to compliment others. This approach will go a long way toward transferring your positive attitude to your students.

- Laughter *is* the best medicine. Kids are funny, and so are you. Have fun, do funny things, notice the funny things your students do. One of my teachers used to play random funny videos throughout the day as we transitioned from one subject or lesson to another, which simply made our time together more enjoyable. Creating opportunities for your students to laugh is one of the fastest ways to foster connection and raise the positive energy in the classroom.

# Attitude Sub-Skill #2: Belief—*something believed; an opinion or conviction*

Students often come into classrooms lacking even a basic belief in themselves and their abilities. Unfortunately, many are equipped with an arsenal of self-limiting and even self-destructive beliefs, which have been unintentionally handed down from those who should whole-heartedly believe in them: their parents, families, and friends. But very often, there are gaping holes in their primary support system. These students desperately need to obtain the self-belief that they simply aren't getting—and perhaps would never get—if they don't receive it from an educator who cares about them.

Did you become a teacher, perhaps in part, because you had that one teacher who impacted your life in a positive way? A teacher who believed in you, spoke words of possibility into you, inspired you, and made you feel like anything was possible?

I had such a teacher. My tenth-grade French teacher, Madame Lawrence, made me feel like anything was possible (and not just mastering French verb tenses or long lists of vocabulary). Thirty years after my last encounter with her, her impact on my life remains.

Developing belief in your students is two-fold: first, it's having belief in yourself (an aspect of leading by example), which, in turn, translates into belief in your students.

These two work in concert to help your students believe in themselves. Ultimately, when you believe in a student and teach that student to believe in themselves, they have the world at their fingertips.

*Everything becomes possible, and nothing is impossible.*

You're going to build *your* self-esteem, and *your* belief in yourself, through the Life S.A.V.E.R.S. Your personal practices of affirmations and visualization, in particular, will shore up any gaps you have and reinforce what's possible for *you*.

In the next chapter, we'll dive more into your Best Behavior, or, said another way, how you can be a role model for your students. What you model for them with intention and purpose becomes a touchstone within themselves, a place they can return to again and again when the going gets tough. They can then rely on it as they deal with life's challenges or when they doubt themselves. Knowing they can and will come out the other side of whatever they encounter— and that they will eventually thrive —is an immeasurable gift.

# Attitude Sub-Skill #3: Character Traits—*features and traits that form an individual*

Every teacher has an innate desire to be great—to impact their students in a positive way; to teach them what they need to learn to be successful, thriving members of society; and to help them be the best they can be both now and in the future.

When teaching is done well, it can be truly satisfying. Positive things happen in classrooms. Students thrive and reach, or even exceed, their potential. You don't have to be "the best teacher," just the best you can be to ensure a positive impact on your students. Embodying the character traits of a legendary teacher, in combination with your A+ Attitude, will ensure your impact on your students lasts long after you've delivered their final grade.

The good news is that you can learn the character traits needed to be just that type of teacher.

## The Character Traits of a Legendary Teacher

- **Effective communication.** You might think the primary character trait for a teacher would be knowledge. However, a teacher's ability to *convey knowledge* stands head and shoulders above what they actually know. It won't matter how much you've learned along the way if you can't teach it to your students in a way they can receive and retain the information, which typically includes delivering it in a way that's enjoyable for them. Always remember that your enthusiasm is contagious!

  Also, keep in mind that story-telling is one of the most effective ways to communicate any lesson so that it's both enjoyable and memorable. Students are more likely to remember the facts when they are delivered via a compelling story.

- **Superior listening.** As the Turkish proverb goes, *If speaking is silver, then listening is gold.* A great teacher strives to hear what a student is actually saying, what they are trying to say, and what they aren't able to say.

Ask quality questions (as well as quality follow-up questions), and then listen actively, empathically, carefully, and without passing judgement.

- **Subject matter knowledge, passion, and mastery.** A teacher is only as good as what they actually know. If you lack knowledge on any of the subjects you teach, then become passionate in your pursuit of more knowledge.
  You can learn through traditional and nontraditional means. Fill yourself with stories, illustrative anecdotes, and relative facts to help the subject come as alive for your students as it is for you.

- **Friendliness and approachability.** Being friendly and approachable is a key element in any teacher's success. If a student is confused, they won't try to eliminate their confusion with a teacher who is crabby, harsh, terse, mean, arrogant or downright unfriendly.
  Develop within yourself an openness, a willingness to help, and a welcoming personality.

- **High expectations (for self and students).** Studies show that when a teacher expects a lot of their students, they have a higher likelihood of seeing results! You need only watch the movies Stand and Deliver, Dead Poets Society, or Lean on Me to see the genuine influence a teacher can have on their students.

Set your own personal standards and share them with your students. Seeing the goals and vision you have for yourself can inspire them.

Set high standards for your students—and be sure to let them know how they can meet or exceed them. Knowing the rules of the game ensures they can win the game. Great teachers share their expectations at the start of the school year and follow them consistently throughout the year. Set three guidelines, such as: *Be respectful. Be prepared. Be on time.* Or, *Respect yourself. Respect others. Respect our school.*

Remember that "schools" and "rules" seem to go hand in hand—the expectation is there. Along with the rules, add your expectations and the commensurate consequences of not following them as well as the rewards they will receive when they meet the challenge successfully.

- **Be purpose driven.** Like everyone, teachers get burned out and forget why they're doing what they're doing. The antidote for burnout is being purpose-driven. Remember *why* you got into teaching, and remind yourself every day with your Life S.A.V.E.R.S. practices.

## Begin with the End in Mind

The second habit in Steven Covey's famed *7 Habits of Highly Effective People* is "Begin with the End in Mind." I believe he means for his readers to spend some time contemplating a few key aspects of their lives from the end of their life—indeed, at the time of their death. In your case, take a moment to imagine your teaching career at the end of your life. When all is said and done, what will you wish had been your legacy, what impact would you want to have had, and who would you want to remember you as *their one teacher who really cared and was intentional about the impact that you made in their life?*

Imagine for a few moments, looking back over your years, and remember students, lessons, and colleagues. Moments and milestones. Good times and memories, and the people who played the key roles in your life and career. I bet you already have a few that, as they float through your mind, make you smile or tear up, or maybe both.

In contemplating this myself, I don't imagine people will talk about how much money I made, what kind of house I lived in, or where I vacationed. I imagine them sharing their favorite memory of me or how I made them feel like anything was possible, gave them food for thought, or comforted them during a seemingly hopeless situation. How I loved my family and friends and readers and clients. That my life made a difference to their lives. *That* is the end I have in mind.

Now it's your turn. Take those beginning thoughts you had a paragraph or two ago and take them further. Grab your journal, and, before you go on to the next chapter, spend some time contemplating the answers to these questions:

- How would you like your students to remember you? List the qualities and character traits that you embody now, as well as those you aspire to represent and instill in your students. (e.g. *Mr./Mrs. _____ always believed in me and assured me that I could do anything I put my mind to...* etc.)

- What types of impacts do you envision your students making in the world, for which you can begin laying the groundwork now? Think of specific students you've had the privilege to teach or are currently teaching, and daydream a bit about what's possible for them.

- If this were your last year, month, or week of teaching, would you be the crabby teacher that should've retired years ago, or are you the teacher who taught with enthusiasm and will be fondly missed by teachers, students, faculty, and parents?

- When will you host your retirement party, and are there any students you would like to attend? Jot down the names of those you want to come back to see you because you made such an impact on their lives.

- What do you envision your legacy to be? Will you be the teacher who helped them overcome a learning disability, or apply for a scholarship, or go into a field they thought might be too difficult?

- How will you continue to learn, grow, and improve, and how will that inspire those around you?

- Does anything else come to mind in terms of the legacy you're committed to leaving?

I think most teachers want to make an impact and be remembered by other teachers and students alike. The good news is that *you get to choose* how you're remembered in five, ten, or even thirty years—that legacy and impact begins and ends with you. And you get to decide right now, today, and every day. Hal and I hope you'll share your vision in The Miracle Morning Community (Facebook Group) and use the Miracle Equation (described in the Bonus Chapter toward the end of this book) to ensure it comes to pass.

Now that we've laid the foundation to your A+ Attitude optimization, let's explore how you're going to, on a daily basis, lead by example by being on your "best behavior." When you're ready, I'll be waiting for you in Chapter 8.

## Meet Legendary Teacher-Contributor
# Koreen Thompson
### Wildwood Montessori, Montevideo, Minnesota, Ages Three to Five

During a challenging season in my life, I sought prayer and picked up the book, *The Miracle Morning*, for the second time. I finally built a daily morning rhythm for myself using the Life S.A.V.E.R.S. After a time, I began to include our children, ages two and four. We exercised together. We read and meditated together. We said affirmations together. I knew my Montessori children needed this rhythm as well. We initiated the Life S.A.V.E.R.S. at Wildwood Montessori in February 2019. At the ages of three to five, they are developing powerful habits to build belief and strengths into their identity.

We started each morning with Exercise. This tended to look like a song, incorporating movement. Our family-style lunch was great for Visualization. I kept it simple, first asking if the children knew what a goal was. The first response from five-year-old Hannah was, "Something you want to learn." Cora, also five, said, "Something hard you want to get good at." Each week, we'd start with a discussion on goals. Since the discussion occurred as a group, the children would often build on each other's comments. For instance, if one said, "I want to be kind," the discussion grew from that theme. In another instance, they all said, "I want to choose challenging works this week." I asked each student questions like, "How did you reach your goal of kindness today?" or "What was something you did today that was challenging?" Lunch was also a good time for me to publicly affirm them for doing a kind or challenging act. The children loved this! We continue it now, and often it creates momentum, with others jumping in to share their observations.

After lunch, we transitioned to Affirmations. I whispered a word to each child. I then asked them to hold that word in their mind and, when called on, say "I am _____." After the child said their word, we repeated the affirmation as a class. A beautiful transition occurred after only a week; the children wanted to create their own affirmations. This was powerful! Now, I often hear a child demonstrating positive self-talk. Recently, a child climbed up a snow hill and yelled, "I am courageous." It is especially inspiring to see more timid children say, "I am brave," and then act on it. Silence is often practiced in a Montessori environment, but the Life S.A.V.E.R.S. experiment encouraged me to approach Silence with greater intention.

Following affirmations, we dove into Reading a growth mindset book. I have one particular book ideal for building on affirmations that's called *I think, I am*. As the children became experienced with their own affirmations, it created greater curiosity for the content in the book, and I started to receive more focused questions regarding the story. Perhaps the most inspiring discovery was witnessing some children Scribing personal affirmations without my direction.

Gifts we can give to children are life-giving habits that equip them to persevere through life's challenges. The Life S.A.V.E.R.S. routine provides a rhythm that can be internalized, even at two years old. As teachers, we can model the Life S.A.V.E.R.S. with grace and love, being careful to guard against demanding or coercive expectation.

## Meet Legendary Teacher-Contributor
# Jodi Fish
### Fourth grade, Indiana

As a fourth-grade teacher at a rural school in Indiana, I was used to students who generally complied with teacher directions and enjoyed my non-traditional teaching style. I worked hard at the beginning of each school year to establish community, routines, rules, and procedures. Rarely did I have to do more than revisit rules and procedures a couple of times during the school year; that is, until this year, when my world turned upside down.

I was desperate to help my students with dysregulated emotions succeed in the classroom. I attended conferences and read professional research. One day, while scrolling through my Facebook feed, I happened upon a post searching for teachers who would be willing to try some focus strategies in their classrooms. I immediately signed up and decided to incorporate the Life S.A.V.E.R.S. framework into my morning meeting. I noticed results immediately.

Although exercise and visualization were the students' most-preferred activities, affirmations and scribing in the form of journaling brought the most dramatic and lasting results. My students with significant adverse childhood experiences (ACEs) were hesitant to participate in the affirmations at first. They had a very fixed mindset, commenting that the affirmations were stupid. I persevered on, hoping that they would eventually participate. After several weeks, affirmations were still not going well. Then, one day during our morning meeting, I changed the delivery from public to more private: from oral to written. That was when the magic happened! All students except one participated! The transformation from a fixed mindset to a more positive, more confident mindset was incredible. The next morning, we drummed our affirmations, whispering them aloud. Later that day, for the first time, I overheard kids discussing the affirmations and believing them! Not only were affirmations changing their ability to focus, they were changing their self-confidence as well!

In addition to the morning meeting, Silence became a very important strategy for refocusing the students in the afternoon. After lunch recess, my students are often restless, and they struggle with transitioning from playtime back to the classroom. Silence paired with breathing intervals gave my students time to calm down and settle into an afternoon of learning. One student commented, "I even use this at home when I am studying for a test. It just helps me calm my brain and learn better."

Incorporating the Life S.A.V.E.R.S. program into our morning meeting caused me to be more intentional about providing my students with a positive, calm start to our day of learning. It helped students let go of emotions and engage in learning activities. I noticed a more intense focus during instructional periods and more independence during work time.

Although I did tweak Life S.A.V.E.R.S. a bit to work for my students, there is only one thing that I would have done differently; I would have begun the S.A.V.E.R.S. on the first day of school!

# — 8 —
# LEGENDARY TEACHER SKILL #2:
## BEST BEHAVIOR

*One looks back with appreciation to the brilliant teachers,
but with gratitude to those who touched our human feelings.
The curriculum is so much necessary raw material,
but warmth is the vital element for the growing plant
and for the soul of the child.*

—CARL JUNG

In a perfect world, your students would come to you from loving, stable homes, with every basic need met, primed and ready to drink in the knowledge you are eager to share. In this perfect world, you would always feel the positive expectation that accompanies the first day of a new school year, filled with enthusiasm and boundless energy.

But we all know that we live in a world that's far from perfect. Truth be told, you may be one of the only positive role models your students have—and may ever have! In fact, for so many students, teachers are their only role models. You may even be more of a *parent* to some of your students than you realize.

In addition, you probably have challenges of your own: your own family with their special needs, perhaps financial pressures, and other challenges that could affect how you show up for your students. If you are burned out, stressed, overwhelmed, or unhappy, your students know it! The underlying message won't be one of encouragement and possibility, but quite the opposite. When you focus on making yourself the best you can be, it will show up in your classroom. You know this to be true: actions speak louder than words.

The *average* teacher, when confronted with student and personal challenges alike, is barely able to make it through the day. Yet you're striving to be a legendary teacher, one who would pick up—and read—a book like *The Miracle Morning for Teachers*, take on daily personal development practices like the Life S.A.V.E.R.S., and bring those same practices into their classroom.

We commend you for this commitment to yourself, your personal development, and giving your best to your students. Here are some quality skills and distinctions to make to model *best behavior* for your students:

# Best Behavior Sub-Skill #1: Acceptance—*the state of being accepted*

The very first piece of being on your best behavior as a teacher is accepting your students as they are, unconditionally, without passing critical judgment or condemnation (which we humans often do to each other, unconsciously). We all respond favorably when someone we admire, are trying to impress, or must please shows that they wholeheartedly accept us. And teachers certainly fit that description for their students. As the majority of people judge themselves—and harshly at that—receiving your acceptance and approval sets the stage for a student's best performance.

A legendary teacher treats every student as if they, too, are legendary. It's a matter of seeing someone as limitless based on their potential, rather than limiting them based on their past.

*Every student needs a champion.*

In life, what you expect is typically what you get. Create an expectation for your students to give their best, and, more often than not, they will rise to the occasion.

Their developing hearts and minds are hungry for a strong and secure environment, including a person (you!) who can see them as an individual while empowering them to believe in themselves and achieve their potential.

- **Get to know your students.** Students learn more, and behave better, when they receive high levels of genuine caring and understanding. Take the time to do exercises that give you a line of insight into their lives outside of your classroom. Really see them as individuals. Treat students as the sensitive and aware human beings they are (because they are always watching, after all). You will accept them at a different level when you truly know them.

- **Listen to your students.** Students can come with expectations of you as their teacher and, when given the opportunity, can provide constructive feedback, input, and information that can help you. It is easy to underestimate how some students, especially those who are younger or less experienced, can help you improve your methods. Learning from your students is a total bonus, and these dynamics go a long way toward your students feeling heard and truly accepted.

- **Be consistent.** Being on your best behavior, *consistently*, provides comfort and certainty. Children often judge an adult's character by their actions; therefore, it is vital that you are consistent in how you treat your students. In your consistency, they will find acceptance (because they will know where they stand, as well as knowing you are open to engaging with them).

- **Encourage and praise them.** Encouraging statements acknowledge the effort students put toward their work and their behavior. Legendary teachers understand the power of praise, although teachers can be predisposed to find errors and make corrections. Learning how to deliver praise might be a challenge, and if so, here's a key opportunity to design affirmations and create visualizations that support you as an expert praise-giver.

Here are the five aspects of effective and positive praise: *authentic, specific, immediate, clean,* and *private.* Make sure your praise is from the heart and is true. You are acknowledging something, and it's important they understand what it is. Also be sure you give the praise as close to the event or action as possible, and it should have no underlying motive or secondary payoff. You're always safe to give praise in private (no other students will get hurt or feel one student is receiving favoritism over another).

The long-term benefits of a student feeling accepted by you—their teacher and someone they look up to—are simply immeasurable. Just know that the results exist, even if you have only anecdotal evidence to prove it.

# Best Behavior Sub-Skill #2: Behavior—*manner of behaving or acting*

Modeling positive behavior in your classroom is significant and sometimes comes down to this simple pidgin-style saying that appeared in American culture in the early 1920s: *monkey see, monkey do.* This refers to *the learning of a process without an understanding of why it works.* In short, your students will do what you *do*, not always what you *say* or what you *say they should do.*

The behavior you model in your classroom, which includes (but is not limited to) your attitude, how you feel about yourself, how you feel about your students, *and* what you say and do, is communicated at deep levels and is not to be underestimated. You know, of course, that your behavior influences your students. And we know, because you're reading this book, that you want to be the kind of teacher whose behavior influences your students in the most positive and beneficial ways possible.

While this isn't a book on specific subjects or curriculum or how to become an expert in what you're teaching—there are plenty of books and opportunities for continued education—you probably know from experience that your passion for your subject matter and knowing it inside and out can inspire your students. Just as one's attitude is contagious, so is enthusiasm. While not every student will take on your love of your particular subject in the way you have, or wish to follow in your footsteps, how you behave each and every day makes a difference. Your attitude will determine whether or not they feel more curious and inspired. And that difference is noticeable. It is calculable; it *matters*.

In addition to the curriculum that you're teaching, you and your behavior give your students a standard to live by. With your every move, expression, and word, you are showing them how to be, not just in your classroom, but out in the world. Your behavior will impact them during the time you have them, and for many years to come.

In addition, how you talk, what you say, your gestures, your habits, and even how you conduct yourself may be their first genuine exposure to things like common sense, manners, common courtesy, and etiquette. These are things they simply may not learn anywhere else because no one at home was able (or willing) to teach what they need to know. It is very possible that their parents don't have these skills or behaviors as part of their repertoire either. You may be more like a parent to many more of your students than you may realize.

None of this is said to put undue pressure on you. It is said that *of whom much is given, much is expected.* And *with great power comes great responsibility.* As a teacher, by virtue of your position, you're given beautiful, open, and young hearts and minds. You have an opportunity to influence them in lasting and positive ways. Isn't that wonderful? I love having the opportunity to make a difference, to give back, and I'm pretty sure if you've read this far, *you do, too.* Otherwise, would you have become a teacher in the first place?

As Hal says, "The greatest gift we can give to those we love and those we lead is to live to our full potential so that we can show them how to live to theirs." Let's make sure you're well-equipped to exhibit the best behavior possible in and out of your classroom.

- **Remember: students learn best from people they like.** This isn't to say every student will like you (or vice versa). When you become *likeable*, the opportunity to make a lasting impact for your students is simply bigger. You're able to connect more quickly and more deeply. The impression you leave is lasting and more durable. Becoming more likeable is simply an inside job: people like people who like themselves, are authentic, and genuinely care about others. Part of your students feeling accepted by you is their knowing you genuinely like and care about them as individuals. And when you like yourself and are comfortable in your own skin, they will know it (even if on a subconscious level).

- **You must put your own oxygen mask on first.** You'll note that your students weren't even mentioned until this third section of the book, because you must take care—*excellent care*—of yourself before you'll have any extra energy to give your students. The hope is, as suggested in the Introduction, that you're reading this as part of your daily reading practice. Perhaps by now you're through a significant part of your initial 30-Day Challenge and well on your way to incorporating each of the Life S.A.V.E.R.S. as part of your Miracle Morning daily ritual.

- **Identify the behavior you expect so you can model it.** You can enhance the impression that your teaching will have when you've taken the time to identify *how* you want to be, *who* you want to be, and *what* kind of teacher you are committed to being. And you need to do this with intention and purpose.

Rather than just winging it, take some time to pencil out some thoughts on how you want to show up. Are you likeable, do you make learning fun, do you prepare lesson plans with passion, do you make an effort to be approachable, and do you strive to be a terrific listener? Is it possible you could craft learning experiences that cater to your students' learning styles and personalities? *Can you?*

Consider what your classroom could be like and remember that the leader—you—sets the tone, tempo, and energy.

As you review the contributions in this book from the teachers who have incorporated the Life S.A.V.E.R.S. with their students and in their classrooms, choose some of the things they did (types of exercise, music, or affirmations, for example) to experiment with in your classroom. It just might take some time to identify the perfect recipe for your ideal classroom—the one in which you're excited to spend your days.

# Best Behavior Sub-Skill #3: Confidence—*belief in oneself and one's abilities*

Developing confidence—in yourself and your students—can and must be one of your main focal points. Just as your behavior influences your students' behavior, your self-confidence and confidence in them will create a clear and visible ripple effect.

## Building Your Self-Confidence

It's very possible that by this point in the book, if you've even just started using affirmations and visualization, you're starting to feel more confident in yourself and your role as a teacher. Fortunately, it doesn't take long before positive self-talk and vivid mental movies begin to take hold and do their great work. As you carry yourself with confidence and sprinkle compliments everywhere, your students' self-confidence will soar also.

- **Do your Life S.A.V.E.R.S. consistently.** Does this go without saying? Maybe. Maybe not. If you've ever done something, discovered it worked, and then found yourself *not* doing it, you're not alone. Keep track of how many days you stick to it, and, when possible, "have a streak." To help you track your progress, you can also download the Miracle Morning 30-

Day Challenge Guide at www.TMMBook.com. Personally, as of this writing, I've been doing the Life S.A.V.E.R.S. for 2,149 days. Have I missed a few days of doing a full morning Life S.A.V.E.R.S. session on occasion? Sure—but I do *at least* five of the S.A.V.E.R.S. every day (meditate, affirmations, visualization, read, and journal), even if it's not an exercise day. Indeed, on some of those days, each of those practices are just one or two minutes, but I'm my best self when I do them. You'll find the same.

- **Learn how to communicate clearly and effectively.** Being an effective communicator isn't just valuable as a teacher, and you'll find that as you focus on getting better and better, other aspects of your life as well as your teaching will improve. If you know you need to become a better communicator, read *How to Win Friends and Influence People* by Dale Carnegie.

- **Stand up and speak up for yourself.** This is pivotal for you and your students! As opportunities arise to stand up for yourself (and they surely will), your students will notice how you handle yourself. Don't be surprised when they take a page out of your handbook and use your words or phrases (and stance and posture) as they are developing their own self-confidence. Say what you mean, mean what you say, and do both with the care and concern we know you have in your heart. *Fierce Conversations* by Susan Scott is an excellent resource for learning to stand up and speak up for yourself, as well as providing tools for having the toughest of tough conversations.

- **Get things done.** Confidence comes from accomplishment. Follow projects through to completion, cross items off your to-do list, and relish in those triumphs. As luck would have it, *Getting Things Done* by David Allen is my go-to resource for when I need to, literally, get things done. It can help you, too!

- **Care what *you* think.** Which is also to say: don't care so much what others think, unless their opinion matters (and they have a right to have an opinion). One of my favorite books on this topic, *Stop Trying So F\*cking Hard*, is actually written by me! I wrote it because I think there's only so much caring one should do for others' opinions (unless you've given them permission to have an opinion *and* share it with you).

- **Do the best you can and strive for improvement.** We are all capable of being great—better, sometimes, then we can possibly imagine. That's what your visualization practice is designed to enhance. Do the best you can imagine and strive to make progress (not to be perfect).

- **Make notes.** In your journal, make a list of your accomplishments—things you are most proud of, moments where you let your light shine, did your best, made a difference. If you don't already have such a list, start one today and add everything you can remember from your life so far. Keep adding until you run out, and then add more as they occur to you and as they happen. Encourage your students to do the same in their journals. Review this list anytime your self-confidence levels drop, and suggest your students do the same. It is sometimes easier to see the mountains we haven't climbed than to look back and appreciate the ones we have. Memorializing and reviewing past accomplishments can provide encouragement and help just when it is needed the most.

You should have the beginnings of how you and your students should conduct themselves in your classroom that will empower and inspire not just your students, but also you (and your fellow teachers, maybe even the administration!). Your best behavior and your A+ Attitude, combined with what's coming up in Chapter 9, collectively make up the trifecta of legendary teaching. When you're ready, turn the page.

## Meet Legendary Teacher-Contributor
# Laura Velez

I discovered *The Miracle Morning* while attempting another business. After fifteen years of teaching English, I considered quitting. The S.A.V.E.R.S. became a self-discovery journey and redefined my purpose. I *love* teaching, and regardless of the downside (even a big one), I wholeheartedly believe it is my calling. Recently, I have observed the stress and turmoil students face today. The expectations set upon them from peers, families, and the education system are enormous, yet we are not equipping them with tools or skills to handle such expectations. Sharing the S.A.V.E.R.S. with my students could help them get closer to their full potential, reach goals others have set for them, and hopefully develop their own goals.

I began by explaining the benefits of the program and how the S.A.V.E.R.S. had helped me and then modeled what we would do for each section to my junior-year students.

Silence was challenging, but keeping the lights off and playing some background meditation music helped. Students individually wrote affirmations on a paper I collected after each session. I encouraged students to write three affirmations, which they could repeat the next day or create new ones. Many changed and aligned their affirmations to specific goals they had for that week or that day. One of the best moments was when a student commented that one of his affirmations had come true.

Surprisingly, visualization was the most complicated section. Some students expressed anxiety about imagining their futures, their "successes." Referring to more specific images such as "what are you wearing when you accomplish ___ goal," "who is next to you," etc., helped them visualize. During exercises, the challenge was that they refused to break a sweat or to move awkwardly in front of their peers. I tried several techniques, from chair yoga to basic calisthenics, but the *best* strategy was playing a song that repeats a specific word. They walked around the classroom, and whenever the buzz word came, they jumped, with their hands in the air. It was *great*!

We used a digital notebook for reading and scribing in order to share the selections quickly and effectively without the hassle of making copies. This allowed students the privacy to interact with the reading at their own pace and respond at their convenience. Selections were short, uplifting, and relevant to issues with which they were coping.

Students loved the Life S.A.V.E.R.S., and as the month went by, they expressed how it had become a part of their routine, and they were looking forward to continuing. I was particularly surprised when one characteristically shy student asked me to keep doing the S.A.V.E.R.S. because he needed the affirmations sheet to focus his day. The last day, I asked students to volunteer as leaders for each section. They were eager to participate, and, more importantly, they knew how to lead their peers in the process. I was impressed, especially with the reading selections and the scribing prompt. One student asked, "What things do you consider important in life, both physical and personal? Who would you be if these were not present?"

# LEGENDARY TEACHER SKILL #3:

## COMMUNITY CREATION

> *The mediocre teacher tells. The good teacher explains.*
> *The superior teacher demonstrates. The great teacher inspires.*
>
> — WILLIAM ARTHUR WARD

L egendary teachers are effective teachers—and their students' behaviors and academic performance reflect it. They create an environment in which their students are excited to come to class and engage in the learning process. They are able to get through to the students who come to them broken, or resistant, or challenged—simply by caring. Legendary teachers create an incredibly positive classroom community, one that fosters a sense of belonging, promotes effective social skills, and encourages high academic achievement. And, legendary teachers form a community of like-minded teachers for support, encouragement, and the exchange of ideas.

Creating these kinds of communities requires proper planning and, usually, lots of practice. Guiding your students to actively participate in class, connect with other students, work collaboratively, and resolve conflicts peacefully requires next-level intention and, sometimes, ninja-level strategy. Finding other teachers who are playing—and performing—at their highest level takes time, patience, and intention.

# Creating Community Sub-Skill #1: Positive Associations—*friendship, companionship, connection; an organization of people with a common purpose*

In addition to setting expectations, establishing classroom rules, and getting to know your students, there are several other interconnected elements to creating a classroom community. These associations will bring out the very best in each student and help to ensure that everyone is successful and happy.

"Associations" in the context of your classroom refers to ensuring students feel both connections to other students as well as a connection to you and what you're teaching. Positive associations ensure they look forward to seeing you, learning from you, and knowing they have at least one friend in the room.

Your classroom can be the one place where your students feel like *everybody knows their name*. It can be a place where they find friends, in addition to knowledge and information. Your classroom becomes a place where they learn and grow and feel cared for as in no other place and by almost no one else.

You can design it to be a place where students learn to associate *learning* with *fun*, *teachers* with *caring*, and *school* with being *safe and sound*.

## Build a Positive Classroom Culture

Having a positive classroom culture is one of the most important elements of a successful learning environment. Effective teachers actively strive to create a classroom culture that encourages individual as well as group participation to ensure every student's success.

It stands to reason that successful students feel connected to school, and this stems from one teacher—you—who makes that connection one of their main focus areas. When students feel their teacher cares about them *as people*, as well as their learning, they are more likely to feel connected.

For this to occur, a teacher must provide the magical combination of high expectations with high levels of support, a focus on positive teacher-student relationships, and physical and emotional safety. Not an easy task in today's high-tech, fast-moving world, but still doable nonetheless.

When students are connected, academic performance improves, violent and destructive incidents reduce, school attendance improves, and more students complete their schooling. They learn better, they are happier, and they have the social connections and skills they will need as they grow into high-functioning members of society.

Evidence shows that when students feel connected, they are less likely to engage in disruptive and/or violent behavior, have less instances of mental health issues (such as depression, anxiety, or suicidal tendencies), drop out less often, are more likely to avoid drug use, and do not engage in early sexual experiences.

*All of this from being a part of a classroom community with a positive feel.* Can you imagine what will happen when you share the Life S.A.V.E.R.S. with your students and arm them with the personal development skills they need to not only achieve their potential but also avoid negative and destructive behaviors?

## Five Ways to Build a Positive Classroom Climate so Your Students Feel Connected to You, Their Fellow Students, and What You're Teaching Them:

1. **Have high expectations.** Yup, the same high expectations mentioned before also factor in to classroom community and culture. You want your students to do well, you expect and encourage them to do so, and you provide appropriate

learning support for all students. The end result is that the students strive to live up to those standards, and in so doing, achieve their best and have increased self-esteem. In turn, their grades and even extra-curricular performances will reflect the standards you set.

2. **Set up a six-minute morning Life S.A.V.E.R.S. practice in your classroom.** Let your students assist in the design and execution of each of the S.A.V.E.R.S. To download a copy of the guide the Legendary Teachers used in their own classroom experiences, visit www.MiracleMorning.com/TeachersGUIDE.com.

3. **Use additional rituals to raise the energy and good vibrations in your classroom.** One example is "High Five Friday," where you stand at your door to high five your students as they enter. Your students will come to look forward to and rely on these activities, and they will look forward to coming to class—or even to school—every single time. After your Monday morning S.A.V.E.R.S. practice, give students who want to share what happened over the weekend a minute to talk. Identify age-appropriate activities you can turn into an ongoing part of your routine.

4. **Focus on fostering friendships between students.** Allocate some of your valuable classroom time and energy to activities that allow your students to bond with each other and let them get to know each other. A great way to do this is to establish a daily (or weekly) "Get to Know Your Classmates" ritual where students pair up and take turns answering a question that you give them, for the purpose of deepening their connections with each other. The questions can either be surface level, or you can challenge your students to go deeper. Some examples of both types of questions that you might consider (depending on the age of your students) are:

- *What is your favorite subject and why?*
- *What is your favorite hobby?*
- *What is your favorite thing to do with your family?*

- *What do you want to be when you grow up?*
- *What are you most excited about right now?*

Or even:

- *What is your biggest fear, and how will you overcome it?*
- *What was the most difficult thing you ever overcame, and what did you learn from it?*
- *What is a problem you see in the world, and how might you fix it?*

Remember that the more we get to know about other people, and the more we're vulnerable with each other, the more human we realize we all are and the more connected we typically feel.

5. **Cultivate positive parental relationships when possible.** Let your students' parents know what your goals are for your classroom and their children your students and ask that they share your high expectations. You can, in many cases, work as a team with the parents to not only educate but also inspire and encourage, which builds a student's self-esteem from multiple points. Remember, parents are their children's first teachers. Send emails directly if you can, or use the smartphone app Seesaw, which enables you to post updates about your students (text, audio, video, and images) and then sends notifications to their parents. Or, you can skip technology altogether and simply put pre-printed notes in their lunch boxes to take home, as a way to communicate with parents and share what their children are working on in the classroom.

Neal Starkman highlighted five teacher attitudes that support connection between them and their students in his book, *Connecting in Your Classroom*. He explained teachers need to be *asset-building, caring, engaging, hard-working,* and *trusting*. When they possess and exude all of these qualities (and do them well), they are poised to produce a strong connection with their students.

If you're not yet sure what behaviors to focus on, here are three questions to get your juices flowing (you can use your Scribing time to come up with effective answers):

- How do I want my students to feel in my classroom?
- How can I help my students develop positive relationships with each other?
- What is the most important thing I want my students to learn this year?

Spend time focusing on these questions, and maybe even brainstorm a few key words, quotes, or phrases that can be an anchor of your classroom culture. Post these phrases up on your classroom walls, talk about them consistently, and look for other ways to instill these core principles in order to create a strong classroom culture.

# Creating Community Sub-Skill #2: Belonging—*someone that belongs*

To paraphrase a popular quote, *Students will forget what you said or did, but they will always remember how you made them feel.* One of the most important things you can do is to make your students feel like they belong.

## Creating a Belonging Atmosphere in Your Classroom

There are three core principles that create *belonging* in your classroom: *relationships, structure,* and *process for progress (not perfection)*. Students who feel connected to others, and form strong relationships, naturally feel more relaxed and included. Having a structure encourages peace of mind; when students know "what's going to happen next," they have lower levels of anxiety. A focus on a process that allows for progress and not an expectation of perfection underscores a student's belief that they belong where they are, which naturally expands their academic and social performance levels.

A simple way to do this is to begin every class by stating something that reassures and reminds everyone that they belong. You might begin class with something along the lines of, "Welcome, everyone. This is a place where you can come as you are, and every single one of you belongs. No one is perfect, but together, as a community, we are all striving to become the best versions of ourselves." Of course, you can modify or add anything to this that helps to set the tone for your intended classroom culture.

## Relationships

The primary principle here is *relationships*. Good relationships between teachers and students, and students with each other, create an effective culture. Like in any relationship, creating a solid connection takes time. However, there are some activities that will support positive attachment faster and easier. Establishing a consistent "Get to Know Your Classmates" ritual, as mentioned above, may be one of the most effective methods. You could add a quick "one-minute share" partner exercise to the end of your six-minute S.A.V.E.R.S. time so students can get to know each other better, or a longer once-a-week group teamwork activity. There are endless ways to encourage relationship-building among your students.

**Opportunity Question:** How can I encourage my students to deepen their relationships with me, our classroom, and other students daily?

## Structure

The second principle is *structure*. Structure includes things such as your classroom's routines, rules, and expectations (which should be easily accessible and understood by everyone, including parents when possible). Also included would be how students are expected to learn and relearn the curriculum. Providing a framework of boundaries, rather than seeking to be in complete and total control, allows students the freedom and autonomy within that framework to work at their best. Facilitation, which encompasses guidance and direction, will help your kids know that you are there to educate as well as oversee what they are doing and maintain order. They will also know they are empowered to handle some challenges on their own and know to ask for help when needed. The added bonus is there will be less "kerfuffling" and more peace in your classroom.

**Opportunity Question:** What are the best ways to establish classroom structure and ensure that my students are all aware of our structure and on the same page?

## Process

The final principle is creating an intentional focus on the *process* of learning rather than being too rigid about goals and outcomes. This is summed up in one of Hal's most popular philosophies: "The key to success is to be committed to the process without being emotionally attached to the results." This can be difficult, especially with outside pressure for higher grades. Students who are solely grade- and goal-focused, particularly those who struggle academically, can quickly become discouraged and give up when their goals go unreached or their grades fall below what they want or need. To provide a classroom culture and community that encourages and inspires, ensure sure your classroom focuses on process (and making progress) *first*— and then performance. Keeping your students' (and your) attention on learning in ways that work best for them, making mistakes, learning from those mistakes, connecting with others, and handling disagreements effectively will allow your students to leave your classroom better than when they arrived. In short, allow them to be on their own journeys, with you as their guide and one who makes the trip a valuable and enjoyable experience for them.

**Opportunity Question:** What are the most effective and positive ways to encourage students to progress while recognizing and rewarding their progress as well as their grades?

This might sound easy, and, of course, these principles are probably all on your radar already. It could be that building relationships, structure, and process led you to teaching in the first place! But these ideals might have gotten lost as you became mired in the pursuit of final exams and end-of-year grades. Revitalizing your focus on these principles, then intentionally and purposefully refocusing on them, often provides a wonderful classroom culture that supports short- and long-term student success.

# Creating Community Sub-Skill #3: Caring—*feel concerned about*

## It's Crucial to Care about Your Students

Of course, it might seem obvious that a teacher would care for his or her students. Caring is an underlying piece of this book, and yet it must be addressed head-on because there are other challenging elements that sometimes test even the most passionate and committed teachers' caring muscles.

You will naturally have your favorite students—the ones who strive to please you, get straight A's, drink in your teachings, and rush to turn in every assignment. Let's face it—those students are easy to care for because they make a teacher's life easier.

It is the students who test limits, make excuses, or are downright disrespectful that make it hard (and sometimes nearly impossible) to care. Consider Hal's philosophy on reserving our judgements of others and loving ALL people unconditionally: "Let us refrain from judging and condemning others, because we simply have no way of knowing that if we had lived their lives, we wouldn't be exactly the same. Instead, take the time to get to know people so you understand where they are coming from, and always come from a place of unconditional love."

As one teacher shared with me, "This is a weird one, caring, because it should be obvious to all and isn't, especially to burned-out teachers. I've had so many students say to me, 'I've never had a teacher who cared before,' or 'I've never felt like anyone was on my side or was cheering me or was rooting for me to succeed.' Again, it is easy to get frustrated with students who seem to not care, to cheat, or to make every excuse under the sun. But you can't let that win! If you care, you'll get so much more mileage out of them. It's astounding what students are capable of when they're motivated by someone believing in them."

There is no "one size fits all" advice, yet there is one fail-proof strategy that can help set you up for success in every area, and that is your Life S.A.V.E.R.S. practice.

You want to be a teacher who is centered and calm, even in the face of the daily chaos and stress that naturally accompanies students. This will come as a result of your daily meditation practice, in addition to the affirmations you craft, write, and say daily that remind you who you want to *be* while you're teaching. Your visualizations can include you at the front of the room sharing your subject passionately, while connecting intentionally with every student. Getting, and staying, in shape will help you physically meet the demands of teaching, while simultaneously giving you the energy you need to care! Let's face it, when we are tired (or hungry, cold, or emotional), doing anything at our best, let alone serving the needs of others, is improbable, if not impossible. Reading daily about your subject—or even a personal development book—and taking notes about what you've read will expand your bandwidth for caring.

And then there are the actual caring pieces: *showing students you care, making it cool for students to care,* and *encouraging them to care, too.*

## How to Show Students You Care

We've covered multiple strategies and approaches for showing students that you care throughout this section, and here are a few others you can implement now and over the long term:

- **Welcome them!** Stand at or outside your door and welcome them by name each morning or class period. Wear the smile suggested earlier, and notice how they are as they enter your room. You might be able to ease any tension, sadness, or other emotion you pick up on by giving them a hug, a high five, and/or a compliment.

- **Engage the unengaged.** Pick one or two students who are less engaged, and focus on them for two or three minutes per day. Ask them to visit with you at your desk for a quick conversation, give them a cool responsibility (like turning in a document at the office—and make sure they know it's a "big deal" and what a wonderful help they are), or write them a note they'll find in their desk, locker, or folder.

- **Debrief.** Before they depart at the end of class, take three minutes to ask for shares to the following questions (or some you write yourself): *What went well today? What was the best thing that happened? Could we do anything differently/better tomorrow?*

- **Attend their extracurricular activities.** Showing up at their dance or piano recitals, games, or other presentations can make a profound and lasting impact. Yes, it will require some of your valuable time, *but you are that teacher, right?* The one who strives not to just teach but to leave a lasting imprint on your students' young and impressionable minds? You don't have to do this often, or even more than once for any one student; just one small effort will be remembered by your students long after you've forgotten them yourself.

- **Pass notes in class.** Keep a notebook handy for the purpose of writing encouraging notes to your students, in addition to report cards, for each grading session. Actively be on the lookout for all sorts of positive actions from your students, and make notes when they do especially well. Write down when you see them treat another student with kindness and respect, when they give above-and-beyond effort, or when you see something about them you can compliment. Catch them doing things well, and acknowledge them for it. They will come to look as forward to your notes as they do your grades.

Hopefully these ideas will have inspired you to come up with others you want to try. Remember: a tiny bit of effort on your part will make a big difference, and each one can inspire your students to think of others in the same wonderful ways. Intentional acts of kindness are contagious, just like attitudes, and you never know what your leading by example will inspire your students to do.

## Make it Cool for Students to Care

One of the concepts I stumbled across in researching for this book was contained in principal and former teacher Todd Whittaker's book, *What Great Teachers Do Differently: 17 Things That Matter Most*, in the chapter entitled, "Make it Cool to Care." He shares:

*My central goal was incredibly simple and incredibly complex. I wanted it to be "cool to care" in my [class]room and in my school. I wanted everyone—every student, every teacher, each staff member, all the parents—to think it was cool to care. Ironically, I don't think I shared this goal with anyone—maybe because it sounded so simple, maybe because people might have scoffed at it, and maybe to improve its chance of becoming reality.*

A classroom culture—and therefore community—that makes a distinct and long-lasting difference is one where the teacher and students care deeply, both about learning and about each other. Anything is possible when this element is embraced wholeheartedly. Issues with missing assignments, failing grades, and discipline are lessened as you encourage your students to strive to be and give their best.

It has been noted that our actions are a direct result of our peer group. When students are involved with a peer group that cares about their academic performance, social activities, and the like, they, too, will care. It will be cool to apply oneself to their studies, engage in extracurricular activities, and even devote their time to volunteer opportunities, when their teachers and peers are doing the same.

Here are a few ways to do just that:

- **Identify opportunities.** Make sure your students know what their opportunities are and how awesome you think it would be if they took advantage of them. Seek until you find just the right fit. Not every student can be the starting quarterback of the football team, but there's a foreign language, a special skill (such as drawing or writing), or some other activity (dance, band, theater, or student government, to name a few) that would help them develop their self-confidence and create their own connections and community outside of your classroom.

- **Keep at it.** My daughter tried karate and dance. Karate was a no, but dance was, and still is, a love of hers. She didn't love sports but became enthralled with being the trainer of the girls' volleyball team, learning how to connect with the other girls as well as learning true responsibility and how to be helpful when it mattered most. Your students will need help, perhaps trying and failing, until they find their groove.

- **Share the rewards.** Let's face it—at the end of each year, the students who did "all of the things," and did them well, are the ones who are honored by their fellow classmates and faculty alike. Again, not the right path for every student, but how many more students would have at least tried to get a 4.0 or become a cheerleader if just one teacher had believed in them enough, and expressed that belief, so that they tried? What might you have done if you had had the focus and attention of a teacher who told you anything was possible?

It will be cool to care when every student in your class (a) knows it is cool to care, (b) sees you care, and (c) knows the other students care, too.

# Bonus Sub-Skill for Creating Community: Build a Like-Minded Community of Teachers

If you believe in the philosophy that says *you are the sum of the five people you spend the most time with*, a quick look around could provide some concerning and not-so-wonderful realizations. You might have an apathetic teacher in the classroom on one side and a burned-out, angry, or fed-up teacher on the other. Your commitment and enthusiasm to be the best teacher you can be might be met with condescending amusement or even cynicism, rather than the unified chorus of, *Let's do this together!* that you would rather hear. What's an aspiring legendary teacher to do?

## Build a Community of Other Legendary Teachers Like You—for You!

One of the greatest opportunities you have is to find other inspired, like-minded teachers who are committed to going above and beyond the minimums that are expected of them. You want to identify those teachers who would be likely to read a book like this and would be excited about the possibility of implementing the Life S.A.V.E.R.S. for themselves and their students, as well as the other best practices we've shared in this book.

The good news is there *are* countless other teachers that fit this description; you just have to know where to look for them (and how to identify and/or help create them)! Dozens of teachers opted in to participating in the group experiment we conducted for this book. Hundreds more read an advanced copy of this book and provided valuable feedback. And finally, there are thousands who are simultaneously reading this book now (and tens and hopefully hundreds of thousands who will read it in the future).

Here are three ways to build your community and find your tribe of teachers:

- Join our Miracle Morning for Teachers Facebook group, and ask if there are teachers in your country, state, or city who are practicing the Life S.A.V.E.R.S. You can join it here: www.TMMTeacherCommunity.com.

- Find an accountability partner for your 30-Day Challenge with your classroom.

- Form *The Miracle Morning for Teachers* book club in your school, school district, or city.

Finding your tribe of inspired, like-minded teachers and building your own community will help you to stay consistent as well as learn strategies and tools to help you become the very best teacher, role model, and person you can be.

## Final Thoughts: Become Legendary

Teaching is an amazing profession, and you're an amazing person just because you chose it as your profession. As we all know, it can be simultaneously challenging, dynamic, energizing, and draining. It is truly rewarding, because the impact teachers make extends far beyond anything you can imagine. I'm sure my French teacher, Madame Lawrence (if she is still alive), has no recollection of me and her impact on me and my life and my love of the French language. But that doesn't make her efforts any less noteworthy or life-changing!

Other teachers, your students, and their parents *will* talk about you. There's no doubt about that. But what are they saying, and what will they say? If you could listen in on their conversations, would what they say make you swell up with pride—or shrink down with embarrassment? Hopefully, it's a lot of the former and none of the latter.

Here's the good news: you get to decide what those conversations will consist of. Perhaps they will wonder how you combined caring and community with curriculum, or discuss how you inspired your students to live up to their full potential, try something new, or even discover their life-long passion.

If you aspire to be an exceptional teacher, if you long to leave a legacy—to become legendary—this reality could be closer than you think. The magical combination of pursuing your passion through teaching and living your values is where you start. Your daily Miracle Morning ritual and the Life S.A.V.E.R.S. are designed to enable you to become the person (and the teacher) that you need to be to create the most extraordinary life—and lasting impact for your students—that both you and they deserve.

Embrace your subject matter wholeheartedly, as the more you geek out on what you're teaching, the more your students will geek out about it. Keep learning, keep growing, and keep improving. Identify and emulate other legendary teachers, and make one of them your mentor if you can. Cultivate an A+ Attitude, as previously discussed, that is impregnable to any negativity, ever.

Finally, stop worrying about what others think about you and what you're doing (unless what they think is *terrific*, then by all means, listen up!), and start living for what you can do for others, including making a positive impact through your example. Remember Hal's words: "The greatest gift we can give to those we love, and those we lead, is to live to our full potential so that we can show them how to live to theirs." Dedicate time to your Miracle Morning practice each day to ensure that you become your best and can give your best to others. Give back, give often, and give freely. Or, as one of my mentors says, "Never miss an opportunity to give, because what you put out always returns multiplied."

Aspiring to be legendary means playing at a level few others ever reach—because they don't even try. You're here, and you've got the tools you need to make it happen. All you've got to do now is *go for it, 100 percent.*

We can't wait to hear all about what happens next!

# Kids Who are Different

*Here's to kids who are different*
*Kids who don't get always get straight A's*
*Kids who have ears*
*Twice the size of their peers*
*And noses that go on for days.*
*Here's to kids that are different*
*Kids they call crazy or dumb*
*Kids who don't fit*
*With the guts and grit*
*Who dance to a different drum*
*Here's to kids who are different*
*Kids with a mischievous streak*
*For when they have grown*
*As history has shown*
*It's their difference that makes them **unique**.*

–DIGBY WOLFE

## Meet Legendary Teacher-Contributor
# Sarah McCravey Martin
### Health Occupations Teacher, Taylor High School, Taylor, Texas

My name is Sarah McCravey Martin, and I am the Health Occupations Teacher at Taylor High School in Taylor, Texas. I teach all levels of high schoolers from ninth grade to twelfth grade, but I felt especially drawn to this opportunity for the seven senior students in my practicum program. I wanted to share the importance of starting your day off on a positive note.

We began by establishing a goal that the students could achieve by the end of the school year. These students will graduate and move on into the real world, so I felt this would be a perfect start for them to think about goals that would benefit them. We discussed the Life S.A.V.E.R.S. on the first day and discussed which of the Life S.A.V.E.R.S. we would do every day.

We would start our morning with one minute of silence and perform a two-minute guided meditation activity to clear the mind of all stress.

The second day we discussed Affirmations, and I gave them the example to use the "I Am alphabet" Honorée had shared with me. For each letter, they would write a positive adjective that describes them, and by reciting this every day, they would feel better about themselves.

The third day we discussed Visualizations, which we incorporated with Meditation. I had them visualize the goals that they chose when we started. By seeing their goals in their minds, they can think positively toward these goals and how it will feel to accomplish them.

On the fourth day, we incorporated exercise, and the girls especially loved this. Every day we alternated between yoga and *Just Dance*, a dancing video game, and they really enjoyed the positive energy they had after they danced to one or two songs a day in the classroom.

As time passed, I noticed the students had a much better start to their day when they practiced each one of the Life S.A.V.E.R.S., especially with the affirmations. One of my students, A.C., made up her own example for the affirmations by using an adjective she chose for herself, and then for each letter she would choose another word that helped describe herself.

Another one of my students has told me that saying the affirmations in the morning helped her to think positively throughout her whole day. Her goal was to exercise more consistently and eat clean, and by thinking positively about working out every day, she was more likely to work out.

Then there was Gaby, who said the positive affirmations have helped her get a good start in the morning, which would help her maintain her goals.

For Rachel, her goal was to make better decisions and to make them more efficiently. By reciting her affirmations and visualizing her goal, she could think positively about deciding.

Then there was Raquel. Her goal was to have a better relationship with her mother, and the affirmations were a big help for her to think positively about her progressing that relationship.

Overall, I feel like my students learned a lot from this experiment. I think it impacted each of them in a positive way, even if it was just one small thing. As their teacher, I truly enjoyed being able to experience this with them and see how, and if, it could change their perspective on the start to their day.

# THE MIRACLE MORNING 30-DAY LIFE TRANSFORMATION CHALLENGE

*An extraordinary life is all about daily,*
*continuous improvements in the areas that matter most.*

—ROBIN SHARMA

Let's play devil's advocate for a moment. Can the Miracle Morning really transform any area of your life, or your students' lives, in just thirty days? Can anything really make that significant of an impact, that quickly? Well, remember that it has already changed the lives of more than a million people in over seventy countries, and if it works for them, it can and will absolutely work for you and your students.

Incorporating or changing any habit typically requires an acclimation period, so don't expect this to be effortless from day one. However, by making a commitment to yourself to stick with it, beginning each day with a Miracle Morning and leveraging the S.A.V.E.R.S. will quickly become the foundational habit that makes all others possible. Remember: *when you win the morning, you set yourself up to win the day.*

While the first few days spent changing a habit may seem unbearable, keep in mind that any difficulties you experience are only temporary (and sometimes non-existent, depending on your level of excitement and commitment). There's a lot of debate about how long it takes to implement a new habit, but the more than one million individuals who have learned how to conquer the snooze button and now wake up every day for their Miracle Morning serve as proof that our powerful three-phase strategy works.

## First You, Then Your Students

To be clear, we suggest *you* first implement your own Miracle Morning 30-Day Life Transformation Challenge for yourself (so that you can experience the life-changing benefits), and then proceed to lead your students through their first 30-Day Challenge, using *The Miracle Morning for Teachers Guide* to walk you through every step of the process.

So, first, let's get you set up for success...

## From Unbearable to Unstoppable:

### The Three-Phase Strategy to Implement Any New Habit in Thirty Days

As you embark on The Miracle Morning 30-Day Life Transformation Challenge, you'll be equipped with arguably the simplest and most effective strategy for implementing and sustaining any new habit in just thirty days. The following strategy will give you the mindset and approach you can take on as you build your new routine.

## Phase One: Unbearable (Days One to Ten)

Phase One is when any new activity requires the most amount of conscious effort, and getting up early is no different. You're fighting existing habits and thought patterns—the very habits and thought patterns that have been entrenched in *who you are* for years.

In this phase, it's a bit of mind over matter—and if you don't mind, it'll definitely matter! The habit of hitting the snooze button and not making the most of your day are the same habits that hold you back from becoming the superstar teacher you have always known you can be. So, dig in and hold strong.

In Phase One, while you battle existing habits, patterns, and even limiting beliefs, you'll find out what you're made of and what you're capable of. You need to keep pushing, stay committed to your vision, and hang in there. Trust me when I say you can do this!

I know it can be daunting on day five to realize you still have twenty-five days to go before your transformation is complete and you've become a bona fide morning person. Keep in mind that on day five, you're more than halfway through Phase One, and the next two phases only get easier from there. Remember: your initial feelings are not going to last forever. In fact, you owe it to yourself to persevere because, in no time at all, you'll be getting the exact results you want as you become the person you've always wanted to be!

## Phase Two: Uncomfortable (Days Eleven to Twenty)

In Phase Two, your body and mind begin to acclimate to waking up earlier. You'll notice that getting up starts to get a tiny bit easier, but it's probably not yet a habit—it's not quite who you are and likely won't feel natural quite yet.

The biggest temptation at this level is to reward yourself by taking a break, especially on the weekends. A question posted quite often in The Miracle Morning Community is, "How many days a week do you get up early for your Miracle Morning?" The answer that's most common from longtime Miracle Morning practitioners is *every single day.* While many *new* practitioners assume that they should take the weekends off (a paradigm that our Monday-Friday work schedule has conditioned us to believe), what they soon find is that each morning you do your S.A.V.E.R.S., your day is significantly better, because *you* are at your best. You might think of this similar to healthy eating; when you eat healthy foods, you feel better, with more energy and mental clarity. On the contrary, when you indulge in junk food, you pay the price. Similarly, every day that you do your S.A.V.E.R.S., you'll feel better, with more energy and mental clarity. Why not give yourself that gift every day?

Once you've made it through Phase One, you're past the hardest period, and it only gets easier from here. So keep going! Why on earth would you want to go through that first phase again by taking one or two days off? Trust me, you wouldn't, so don't!

## Phase Three: Unstoppable (Days Twenty-One to Thirty)

Early rising is now not only becoming a habit, it has literally become part of *who you are*—part of your identity. Your body and mind will have become accustomed to your new way of being. These next ten days are important for cementing the habit in yourself and your life, since you'll be gaining more and more confidence in your ability to follow through with your Miracle Mornings *and* you'll be getting more competent and effective at each of the S.A.V.E.R.S.

As you engage in the Miracle Morning practice each day, you will also develop an appreciation for the three distinct phases of habit change. A side benefit is that you will realize you can identify, develop, and adopt any habit that serves you—including the habits of legendary teachers that we have included in this book.

Now that you've learned the simplest and most effective strategy for successfully implementing and sustaining any new habit in thirty days, you know the mindset and approach that you need to complete The Miracle Morning 30-Day Transformation Challenge. All that's required is for you to commit to getting started and following through.

## Consider the Rewards

When you commit to The Miracle Morning 30-Day Life Transformation Challenge, you will be building a foundation for success in every area of your life, for the rest of your life. By waking up each morning and practicing the Miracle Morning, you will begin each day with extraordinary levels of *discipline* (the crucial ability to get yourself to follow through with your commitments), *clarity* (the power you'll generate from focusing on what's most important), and *personal development* (perhaps the single most significant determining factor in your success). Thus, in the next thirty days, you'll find yourself quickly *becoming the person* you need to be to create the extraordinary levels of personal, professional, and financial success you truly desire and deserve.

You'll also take the Miracle Morning from a concept that you may be excited (and possibly a little nervous) to "try" and transform it into a lifelong habit—one that will continue to develop you into the person you need to be to create the life you've always wanted. You'll take fulfilling your potential to the next level and see results in your life far beyond what you've ever experienced before. And you'll set yourself up to lead by example for your students—because, remember, the greatest gift you can give to those you love, and those you lead, is to live to your full potential so that you can show them how to live to theirs.

In addition to developing successful habits, you'll also be developing the *mindset* you need to improve your life—both internally and externally. By practicing the Life S.A.V.E.R.S. each day, you'll be experiencing the physical, intellectual, emotional, and spiritual benefits of *Silence*, *Affirmations*, *Visualization*, *Exercise*, *Reading*, and *Scribing*. You'll immediately begin to feel less stressed, more centered, more focused, happier and more excited about your life. You'll be generating more energy, clarity, and motivation to move toward your highest goals and dreams (especially those you've been putting off far too long).

Remember, your life situation will improve to the degree that you commit to developing yourself into the person you need to be to improve it. That's exactly what these next thirty days of your life can be—a new beginning, and a new you.

## You Can Do This!

If you're feeling nervous, hesitant, or concerned about whether or not you will be able to follow through with the Miracle Morning for thirty days, relax—it's completely normal to feel that way. This is especially true if waking up in the morning is something you've found challenging in the past. It's not only expected that you would be a bit hesitant or nervous, but it's actually a very good sign! It's a sign that you're *ready* to commit—otherwise you wouldn't be nervous.

Here we go…

**Step One:** Get The Miracle Morning 30-Day Transformation Challenge Fast Start Kit

Visit www.TMMBook.com to download and print your free Miracle Morning 30-Day Life Transformation Challenge Fast Start Kit—complete with the exercises, affirmations, daily checklists, tracking sheets, and everything else you need to make starting and completing The Miracle Morning 30-Day Life Transformation Challenge as easy as possible. Please take a minute to do this now.

**Step Two:** Plan Your First Miracle Morning for Tomorrow

If you haven't already began, commit to (and schedule) your first Miracle Morning as soon as possible—ideally *tomorrow*. Yes, actually write it into your schedule, and decide where it will take place. Remember, it's recommended that you leave your bedroom and remove yourself from the temptations of your bed altogether. My Miracle Morning takes place every day on my living room couch while everyone else in my house is still sound asleep. I've heard from people who do their Miracle Morning sitting outside in nature, such as on their porch or deck, or at a nearby park. Do yours where you feel most comfortable, but also where you won't be interrupted.

**Step Three:** Read Page One of the Fast Start Kit and Do the Exercises

Read the introduction in your Miracle Morning 30-Day Life Transformation Challenge Fast Start Kit, follow the instructions, and complete the exercises. Like anything in life that's worthwhile, successfully completing The Miracle Morning 30-Day Life Transformation Challenge requires a bit of preparation. It's important that you do the initial exercises in your Fast Start Kit (which shouldn't take you more than an hour), keeping in mind that your Miracle Morning actually begins with the *preparation* that you do the day (or night) before to get yourself ready mentally, emotionally, and logistically for the Miracle Morning. Keep in mind that if hitting the snooze button has been a challenge for you in the past, your preparation will likely include following the five simple steps outlined in "Chapter 2: It Only Takes 5 Minutes to Become a Morning Person."

**Step Four:** Get an Accountability Partner (Recommended)

The overwhelming evidence for the correlation between success and accountability is undeniable. While most people resist being held accountable, it is hugely beneficial to have someone who will hold us to higher standards than we'll hold ourselves to. All of us can benefit from the support of an accountability partner, so it's highly recommended—but definitely not required—that you reach out to someone in your circle of influence (a fellow teacher, family member, friend, significant other, etc.) and invite them to join you in The Miracle Morning 30-Day Life Transformation Challenge.

Not only does having someone to hold us accountable increase the odds that we will follow through, but joining forces with someone else is simply more fun! Consider that when you're excited about something and committed to doing it on your own, there is a certain level of power in that excitement and in your individual commitment. However, when you have someone else in your life—a friend, family member, or co-worker—and they're as excited about it and committed to it as you are, it's much more powerful.

Call, text, or email one or more people today, and invite them to join you for The Miracle Morning 30-Day Life Transformation Challenge. The quickest way to get them up to speed is to send them the link to **www.MiracleMorning.com** so they can get free and immediate access to *The Miracle Morning Fast Start Kit:*

⇨ **The FREE Miracle Morning Video training**

⇨ **The FREE Miracle Morning Audio training**

⇨ **Two FREE Chapters of *The Miracle Morning* book**

It will cost them nothing, and you'll be teaming up with someone who is also committed to taking their life to the next level, so the two of you can support, encourage, and hold each other accountable.

**IMPORTANT:** Don't wait until you have an accountability partner on board to do your first Miracle Morning and start the 30-Day Life Transformation Challenge. Whether or not you've found someone to embark on the journey with you, I still recommend scheduling your first Miracle Morning to take place tomorrow—no matter what. Don't wait. You'll be even more capable of inspiring others to do the Miracle Morning once you've already experienced a few days of it. Get started. Then, as soon as you can, invite a friend, family member, or fellow teacher to join you.

## Are You Ready to Take *Your* Life to the Next Level?

What is the next level in your personal or professional life? Which areas need to be transformed in order for you to reach that level? Give yourself the gift of investing just thirty days to make significant improvements in your life, one day at a time. No matter what your past has been, you *can* change your future, by changing the present.

## Meet Legendary Teacher-Contributor
# Yanina Cuesta
### English as a New Language, Ninth to Twelfth Grades

I start every morning meditating, and this has provided great peace in my life. I have been eager to introduce my students to this process, and sharing the Life S.A.V.E.R.S. with my students seemed perfect.

Before the month started, I had the students formulate a goal(s) they wanted to really focus on. I wanted the students to not be impeded by how much English they understood but rather to focus on the experience of the Life S.A.V.E.R.S., so I created a bilingual journal that would have each of the steps listed, as well as questions to guide their scribing.

I would have liked to do this program with students at the beginning of the day, but my only stand-alone class is at the end of the day. This added a different and interesting dimension to some of the steps. They really enjoyed silent time, because it afforded them the opportunity to quiet their minds enough to be open to new things. The first week, I guided them through some breathing exercises to focus them, but then we listened to some gentle meditation music.

The journal pages provided a section to write their affirmations. After reading some posts on the Facebook page, I think I would have tried the say-repeat method and have them said aloud, because a student admitted to using this time to try and sleep a little longer.

Visualization was the hardest for me to facilitate. I guided the students with the prompts our guide suggested in both English and Spanish but didn't really change beyond that. To my surprise, several of the students indicated that this was their favorite activity of the program. In their words:

"Me ayudó a visualizar mi futuro."—Brayan Garzón (Translation: "It helped me visualize my future.")

"Visualizar a cerca de mi vida, pensar en lo que más quiero en mi vida, a ver que pasos puedo hacer para empezar mi meta."—Dina Isabel Palacios (Translation: "Visualize my life and think about what I really want in my life, to see what steps I can take to begin my goal.")

The exercise portion was the least liked by the students, which I think was due to their age (fifteen- to twenty-year-olds) more than anything else. Slow movements and stretches worked better than jumping around, such as jumping jacks or running in place. The students mentioned that "slow and gentle was more in the flow of the previous steps." The reading portion went well. We used motivational stories from the web that I translated into Spanish, providing students both language copies. Their responses indicated that they were thoughtful when responding. They rarely chose the self-reflection questions.

At the end of the month, we discussed the benefits of self-reflection for growth. I think it will take my students a lot more work to get there, but we'll continue to work on it.

# A SPECIAL INVITATION FROM HAL

## (JUST IN CASE YOU MISSED IT THE FIRST TIME.)

Since 2012, readers and practitioners of *The Miracle Morning* have co-created an extraordinary community. Consisting of over 200,000 like-minded individuals from around the world, these people wake up each day and dedicate time to fulfilling the unlimited potential that is within all of us, while contributing to the collective Miracle Morning Mission—to *elevate the consciousness of humanity, one morning at a time.*

As the author of *The Miracle Morning*, I felt that it was my responsibility to create an online community where readers could come together to connect, discuss the book, share best practices, find an accountability partner, and support each other. I created The Miracle Morning Community as a Facebook group, since most of us are already on Facebook. This way you don't have to log into an additional website.

However, I had no idea that The Miracle Morning Community would grow to over 200,000 members and become one of the most positive, engaged, and supportive online communities in existence—but it has.

## Join The Miracle Morning Community on Facebook

I'm constantly astounded by the caliber and the character of our member community, which presently includes people from over 70 countries and is growing daily. I invite you to join us at **www.MyTMMCommunity.com** (just make sure you're logged into Facebook).

More recently, the teachers who contributed to this book (you'll find many of their stories at the end of each chapter) are supporting each other in their own online community (for teachers only), where you can connect with other like-minded teachers who are reading and practicing *The Miracle Morning for Teachers* and implementing the Life S.A.V.E.R.S. with their students.

## Join *The Miracle Morning for Teachers* Community on Facebook:

To connect with other like-minded teachers, learn what's working, ask specific questions, share ideas and more, visit **www. TMMTeachersCommunity.com** (again, be sure that you're logged into your Facebook account to join the communities).

While you'll find many who are just beginning their Miracle Morning journey, you'll find even more who have been at it for years and who will happily share advice, support, and guidance to accelerate your success.

I'll be helping to moderate both communities and checking in regularly, so I look forward to seeing you there!

With love & gratitude,

–Hal

# — CONCLUSION —

## LET TODAY BE THE DAY
## YOU GIVE UP WHO YOU'VE BEEN
## FOR WHO YOU CAN BECOME

*Every day, think as you wake up, "Today, I am fortunate
to have woken up, I am alive, I have a precious human life,
I am not going to waste it. I am going to use all my energies
to develop myself, to expand my heart out to others.
I am going to benefit others as much as I can."*

—DALAI LAMA

*Things do not change. We change.*

—HENRY DAVID THOREAU

Where you are is a result of who you *were*, but where you go from here depends entirely on who you choose to be, from this moment forward.

Now is your time. Decide that today is the most important day of your life, because it is who you are becoming now—based on the choices that you make and the actions that you take—which will determine who and where you are going to be for the rest of your life. Don't put off creating and experiencing the life—happiness, health, wealth, success, and love—that you truly want and deserve.

As one of my mentors, Kevin Bracy, always urged: "Don't wait to be great." If you want your life to improve, you have to improve yourself, first. With or without an accountability partner, commit to completing your 30-Day Challenge so that you will immediately begin accessing more of your potential than you ever have before. Imagine… just one month from now, you will be well on your way to transforming every area of your life.

## Let's Keep Helping Others

May I ask you a quick favor?

If this book has added value to your life, if you feel like you're better off after reading it, and if you see that the Miracle Morning can be a new beginning for you to take any—or every—area of your life to the next level, I'm hoping you'll do something for someone you care about:

Give this book to them. Let them borrow your copy. Ask them to read it, so that they have the opportunity to transform their life for the better. Or, if you're not willing to give up your copy quite yet because you're planning on going back and re-reading it, maybe you can get them their own copy. It could be for no special occasion at all, other than to say, "Hey, I love and appreciate you, and I want to help you live your best life. Read this."

If you believe, as I do, that being a great friend, family member, or colleague is about helping your friends and loved ones to become the best versions of themselves, I encourage you to share this book with them.

Together, we are truly elevating the consciousness of humanity, one morning at a time.

Thank you so much.

# — BONUS CHAPTER —

## THE MIRACLE EQUATION

*If you want to experience prosperity at a miraculous level,*
*you must leave behind your old ways of thinking*
*and develop a new way of imagining*
*what's possible for you to experience in your life.*

—DR. WAYNE DYER

You now have a proven process for daily personal development that will enable you to develop the internal qualities and characteristics you need in order to achieve everything you want for your life. However, consider that personal development, in and of itself, doesn't actually produce the achievements. In other words, theoretically, one could dedicate time each day to their Miracle Morning practice but still shy away from pursuing their biggest and most meaningful goals. Thus, in addition to a process for *personal development*, it's equally important that we have a strategy for *goal achievement*.

To make this leap, there is one more helpful tool for you to add to your toolbox, and it's called the *Miracle Equation.*

The Miracle Equation is the underlying strategy that the world's most successful people—I'm talking about humanity's most prolific achievers and creators—have used for centuries to overcome their internal conflicts and create extraordinary outcomes. And it's the formula that I've used to turn my personal development into tangible, measurable results and to realize my full potential in all areas of my life. And it has to do with how you approach your goals.

One of my mentors, Dan Casetta, taught me: "The purpose of a goal isn't to hit the goal. The real purpose is to develop yourself into the type of person who can achieve your goals, regardless of whether you hit that particular one or not. It is who you become by giving it everything you have until the last moment—regardless of your results—that benefits you the most."

Each time you make a decision to pursue and fully commit to a deeply meaningful, highly challenging, and sometimes even seemingly unattainable goal—even though the possibility of failure is present—you give yourself the opportunity to continually evolve and elevate what you're capable of. When your objective is truly significant, it will require you to dig deep and find out what you are really made of!

## You're Only Two Decisions Away from Everything You Want

As with any worthwhile endeavor, you need to make decisions related to achieving your goals. Beyond merely setting a deadline and making a plan, ask yourself, "If I were to achieve my goal on the deadline, what decisions would I have to make and commit to in advance?"

When we study the world's most prolific achievers, innovators, philanthropists, athletes, and just about anyone else who has made a significant contribution to the world, we see that they have done so by establishing and maintaining *unwavering faith* that they could and then putting forth *extraordinary effort* until they did. When you consistently maintain unwavering faith and put forth extraordinary effort over an extended period of time, you cannot fail. You may stumble, you may experience setbacks, but your success will ultimately move from possible . . . to probable . . . to inevitable.

You'll find that, whatever the goal, the two decisions that determine your outcome are *always the same*. And these two decisions form the basis for the Miracle Equation.

## The First Decision: Unwavering Faith

The first time I discovered and used the Miracle Equation, I was twenty years old and striving to achieve an almost impossible sales goal, attempting to set a record that would surpass anything anyone had done in the fifty-year history of the company I worked for. Though this example comes from my sales experience, I'll show you how it applies within the context of any goal you have.

This was a stressful time, as I was naturally facing fear and self-doubt. However, my thought process about the goal forced me to an important realization: to achieve the seemingly impossible, I would have to establish and maintain unwavering faith, every day, *regardless of my results*.

As is true for most any major goal we pursue, I knew that there would be moments when I would doubt myself and times when I would likely be so far off track that the goal might no longer seem achievable. It would be in those moments when I would need to override my fear with faith.

To keep that level of faith in those challenging moments, I consistently repeated and lived by what I call my Miracle Mantra:

*I am committed to maintaining unwavering faith that I will reach my goal and putting forth extraordinary effort until I do, no matter what. There is no other option.*

Repeating this mantra over and over again (especially when I encountered obstacles or doubted myself) enabled me to establish the unwavering faith that I could achieve any goal I set. Even more importantly, it reinforced my commitment to give it everything I had until the last possible moment, regardless of my results along the way. And that is the type of faith—particularly unwavering faith in one's self—that is embodied by the world's happiest and most successful people, in all walks of life.

Understand that maintaining unwavering faith isn't *normal*. In fact, it's abnormal. It defies human nature. It's not what most people do. When it doesn't look like the desired result is likely, most people give up the faith that it's possible. For example, in sports, when the game is on the line, a team is down on the scorecards, and there are only seconds left, it is only the top performers—the Michael Jordans of the world—who, without hesitation, tell their team, "Give me the ball."

The rest of the team breathes a sigh of relief because they no longer have to fear that they may miss the game-winning shot. All the while, Michael Jordan maintained the faith that he could make every shot he took, even though the possibility of missing always exists. And although Michael Jordan did miss twenty-six game-winning shots in his career, he kept shooting and became one of the greatest basketball players of all time, because his faith that he could make every single one never wavered.

Elite athletes maintain unwavering faith that they can make every shot and win every game, even though no one makes every shot or wins every game. That faith—and the faith you need to develop—isn't based on probability. It comes from a whole different place. No matter how many shots you miss or times you fail, you must tell yourself what Michael Jordan tells himself: *It doesn't matter how many times I've missed (a.k.a. "the past"), I have faith that I can make the next one.*

That is the first decision that limitless individuals make—to live with a mindset of *unwavering faith*, and it's yours for the making, too.

When you're working toward a goal, and you're not on track, what is the first thing that goes out the window? The faith that the outcome you want is possible. This usually causes our self-talk to turn negative and self-limiting: I'm not on track. It doesn't look like I'm going to reach my goal. Oh well, I guess it wasn't meant to be. And with each passing moment, your faith in yourself and what's possible wavers.

You don't have to settle for that. You have the ability and the choice to maintain that same unwavering faith that the world's most effective people maintain, regardless of your results. In the darkest moments, it's normal to question yourself and wonder if everything is going to turn out okay, which is why you must make the conscious decision—over and over again—to reinforce your faith that you can overcome, accomplish, and create anything that you're committed to.

And any time you encounter an obstacle, or self-doubt starts creeping in, repeat the Miracle Mantra to yourself:

*I am committed to maintaining unwavering faith that I will reach my goal and putting forth extraordinary effort until I do, no matter what. There is no other option.*

Then, it's simply a matter of upholding your integrity and doing what it is that you've committed to do to achieve your goal.

An elite athlete may be having the worst game ever, where it seems like in the first three-quarters of the game, they can't make a shot to save their life. Yet, their faith doesn't waver, and they keep taking shot after shot. And in the fourth quarter, right when the team needs them, they start making those shots. They keep asking for the ball, because they always have faith in themselves. In the fourth quarter, it's not uncommon to see one of our beloved top performers score more shots than they made in the first three quarters combined.

Why? They have conditioned themselves to have unwavering faith in their talents, skills, and abilities, regardless of what's happened until this point.

And…

They combine their unwavering faith with the second half of the Miracle Equation: *Extraordinary Effort.*

## The Second Decision: Extraordinary Effort

When you allow your faith to go out the window, effort almost always follows right behind it. *After all,* you tell yourself, *what's the point in even trying to achieve my goal if it doesn't look like it's possible?*

Suddenly, you find yourself wondering why you even considered such an outlandish goal for yourself in the first place.

I've been there many times, feeling deflated and thinking, *What's the point of even trying?* And you might easily think, There's no way I can make it.

That's where extraordinary effort comes into play. You need to stay focused on your original goal. You need to connect to the vision you had for it, that big *why* in your heart and mind when you set the goal in the first place.

Like I did, you need to reverse engineer the goal. Fast forward to a vision of you having already achieved your goal and ask yourself, *To have successfully achieved my goal, what would I have done? What would I have needed to do?*

The answer to those questions determines your *process*, and every desired result we have is always preceded by a process that is necessary to producing the result. For example, if your desired result is to lose weight, the process that is required almost always involves both limiting your caloric intake and exercising to ensure that you are burning more calories than you take in. If your desired result is to achieve financial freedom, your process will involve increasing your income so that it exceeds your expenses. Back when I was in sales, my desired results ("sales goals") were determined by my process of making calls to prospective customers. The more I engaged in my process (i.e. the more calls I made), the closer I inched toward my desired result.

Your Extraordinary Effort *is* your commitment to your process. What will make your effort "extraordinary" is simply that you maintain that effort consistently, over an extended period of time. I know that sounds pretty ordinary, but when you consider that few people actually maintain consistent effort over an extended period of time, doing so will enable you to rise above what most people do so that you can consistently create tangible, measurable miracles.

Allow me to introduce you to your edge—the strategy that will move your goals from possible, to probable, to inevitable.

# The Miracle Equation

*Unwavering Faith + Extraordinary Effort = Miracles*

It's easier than you think. The secret to maintaining unwavering faith is to recognize that it's a mindset and a *strategy*—it's not concrete. In fact, it's elusive. You can never make *every* sale. No athlete makes *every* shot. You must program yourself automatically to have the unwavering faith to drive you to keep putting forth the extraordinary effort—regardless of the results.

Remember, the key to putting this equation into practice, to maintaining unwavering faith in the midst of self-doubt, is the Miracle Mantra:

*I am committed to maintaining unwavering faith that I will reach my goal and putting forth extraordinary effort until I do, no matter what. There is no other option.*

Once you set a goal, put that goal into the Miracle Mantra format. Yes, you're going to say your affirmations every morning (and maybe every evening, too). But all day, every day, you're going to repeat your Miracle Mantra to yourself: during your Miracle Morning and while you're on the treadmill, driving in the car, taking a shower, standing in line at the grocery store—in other words: *everywhere you go.*

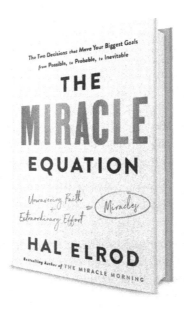

Your Miracle Mantra will fortify your faith and reinforce the self-talk you need to continue moving forward and making progress, day after day, *until* you achieve each of your most meaningful goals.

After nineteen years of living and teaching the Miracle Equation (long before *The Miracle Morning* was even an idea), I finally convinced a publisher to let me write a book about it!

*The Miracle Equation: The Two Decisions that Move Your Biggest Goals from Possible, to Probable, to Inevitable* is designed to be the perfect complement to *The Miracle Morning* (TMM). While TMM gives you a plan for your "personal development," *The Miracle Equation* complements TMM by giving you a proven, step-by-step formula for your "goal achievement."

AND... you can now download a free sneak peek of the book at TheMiracleEquation.com. I sincerely hope it helps you to move *your* biggest goals from possible...to inevitable!

With love & gratitude,

–Hal

# ABOUT THE AUTHORS

**HAL ELROD** is on a mission to *elevate the consciousness of humanity, one morning, one person at a time.* As creator of one of the fastest-growing and most-engaged online communities in existence and author of one of the highest-rated, best-selling books in the world, *The Miracle Morning*—which has been translated into 34 languages, has over 2,000 five-star Amazon reviews and is practiced daily by over 500,000 people in 70+ countries—he is doing exactly that.

What's remarkable is that Hal actually died at age twenty. His car was hit head-on by a drunk driver at seventy miles per hour, his heart stopped beating for six minutes, he broke eleven bones, and he woke up after being in a coma for six days to be told by his doctors that he would never walk again.

Then, in November of 2016, Hal nearly died again—his kidneys, lungs, and heart were all on the verge of failing, and he was diagnosed with a rare and very aggressive form of cancer and given a 20-30 percent chance of surviving. After enduring the most difficult year of his life, Hal is now in remission and grateful to be living his mission alongside his wife and their two children in Austin, Texas.

For more information on Hal's keynote speaking, live events, books, and the soon-to-be-released documentary, *The Miracle Morning* (movie), visit HalElrod.com.

**HONORÉE CORDER** is an executive and strategic book coach, TEDx speaker, and the author of dozens of books including *You Must Write a Book, The Prosperous Writer book series, Like a Boss* book series, *Vision to Reality, Business Dating, The Successful Single Mom* book series, *If Divorce is a Game, These are the Rules, The Divorced Phoenix*, and many more. Additionally, she is co-creator of *The Miracle Morning* book series with Hal Elrod. Honorée passionately coaches business professionals, writers, and aspiring non-fiction authors who want to publish their books to bestseller status, create a platform, and develop multiple streams of income in her You Must Write a Book LIVE Coaching Course, and runs the Empire Builders Mastermind. She does all sorts of other magical things, and her badassery is legendary. You can find out more at HonoreeCorder.com.

# THE MIRACLE MORNING SERIES

**THE JOURNAL**

**FOR SALESPEOPLE**

**FOR REAL ESTATE AGENTS**

**FOR NETWORK MARKETERS**

**FOR WRITERS**

**FOR ENTREPRENEURS**

**FOR PARENTS & FAMILIES**

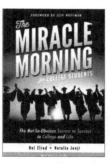

**FOR COLLEGE STUDENTS**

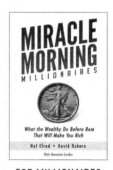

**FOR MILLIONAIRES**

# THE MIRACLE MORNING SERIES

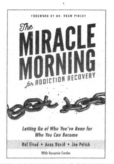

FOR ADDICTION RECOVERY

FOR COUPLES

# COMPANION GUIDES & WORKBOOKS

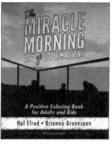

ART OF AFFIRMATIONS

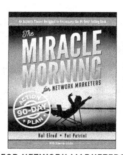

FOR NETWORK MARKETERS
90-DAY ACTION PLAN

FOR SALESPEOPLE
COMPANION GUIDE

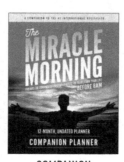

COMPANION
PLANNER

FOR COLLEGE STUDENTS
COMPANION PLANNER

# BOOK HAL to SPEAK

*"Bringing Hal in to be the keynote speaker at our annual conference was the best investment we could have made."* —**Fidelity National Title**

*"Hal was the featured keynote speaker for 400 of our TOP sales performers and executive team. He gave us a plan that was so simple, we had no choice but to put it in action immediately."* —**Art Van Furniture**

*"Hal received 9.8 out of 10 from our members. That never happens."* —**Entrepreneur Organization (NYC Chapter)**

**Book Hal as your keynote speaker and you're guaranteed to make your event highly enjoyable and unforgettable!**

For more than a decade, **Hal Elrod** has been consistently rated as **the #1 keynote speaker** by meeting planners and attendees.

His unique style combines inspiring audiences with his unbelievable TRUE story, keeping them laughing hysterically with his high-energy, stand-up-comedy-style delivery, and empowering them with actionable strategies to take their *RESULTS* to the *NEXT LEVEL*.

*For more info visit* **www.HalElrod.com**